Marianne van Velzen was born in the Netherlands but grew up in Australia. In her late teens she emigrated back to Europe and later became a journalist. She has a life-long interest in Australia and is the author of *Call of the Outback*, published in 2016, and *Bomber Boys*, published in 2017.

MISSING in ACTION

Also by Marianne van Velzen

*Call of the Outback: The remarkable
story of Ernestine Hill, nomad, adventurer and trailblazer*

*Bomber Boys: The extraordinary adventures of a group of
airmen who escaped the Japanese and became the RAAF's
celebrated 18th Squadron*

MARIANNE VAN VELZEN

MISSING in ACTION

Australia's World War I Grave Services, an astonishing story of misconduct, fraud and hoaxing

ALLEN&UNWIN
SYDNEY•MELBOURNE•AUCKLAND•LONDON

Allen & Unwin
83 Alexander Street
Crows Nest NSW 2065
Australia
Phone: (61 2) 8425 0100
Email: info@allenandunwin.com
Web: www.allenandunwin.com

A catalogue record for this book is available from the National Library of Australia

NATIONAL LIBRARY OF AUSTRALIA

ISBN 978 1 76063 280 9

Map by MAPgraphics
Set in 11.5/18 pt Sabon Pro by Midland Typesetters, Australia
Printed in China by C&C Offset Printing Co., Ltd.

10 9 8 7 6 5 4 3 2

To Richard Walsh
who pointed the way

CONTENTS

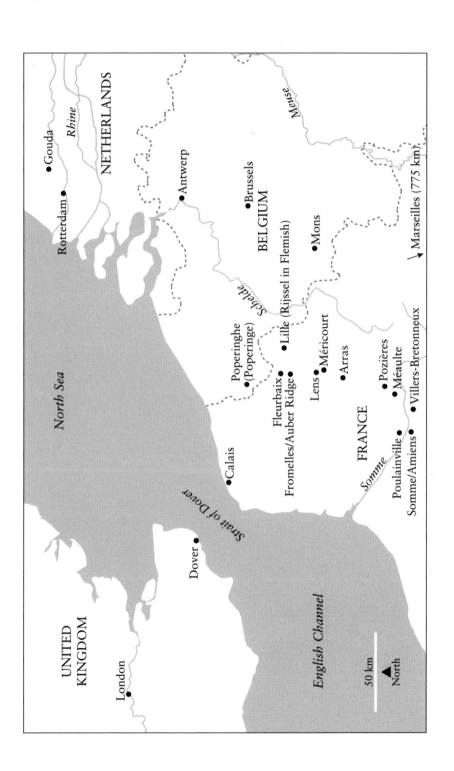

IN THE BEGINNING

Englishman Fabian Ware was 45 when the war broke out in 1914. He had studied in London and Paris, obtaining a bachelor's degree in science. As the war spread across the world with apocalyptic ferocity, he felt the need to be somehow involved.

At the start, he envisaged a role for himself in battle. He had no idea what this role might be and how it would develop so he started at the logical place: he attempted to join the troops. There was only one problem: the age limit was between 18 and 38.

As far as Ware was concerned, it was a minor detail. The age limit for Australians had gone from 38 to 45, and in some cases men even older had been known to enlist. Ware couldn't imagine why this could not also apply for the English service. He was sure that his experience of life and knowledge of the French language would make up for his excess of years.

To no one's surprise but his own, the British Army rejected him, categorising him as too old. After his services had been kindly but decisively refused, friends who knew him realised that he would never be content to sit back comfortably and watch the world burn. Taking it easy had never been Fabian Ware's way.

One afternoon, while discussing the war with his friend Lord Milner, Ware learned that the British Red Cross was looking for volunteers to help with its work on the battlefields in France. Milner had ties to the Red Cross and, if Ware was interested in an appointment, his friend would put in a good word or two in his favour.

Ware had no idea how this would turn out, but he decided to apply. There appeared to be no age limit and so, with a little help from Lord Milner, Fabian Ware was appointed head of the Red Cross Mobile Ambulance Unit in France. Just a few months later, in September 1914, Ware found himself making his way across the Channel to Calais.

Nothing had prepared him for the horror he encountered on the front line of the battlefields in France. Driving his Red Cross car to the front he came across destroyed villages, dead livestock and shell-shocked soldiers returning from battle. The lack of any emotion in those young boys' eyes struck Ware. They appeared to walk along like battalions of living dead. The sheer number of casualties and deaths was staggering and the strategy in place to collect the wounded was shoddy at best. The French Army did what it could, but the maimed and dying soldiers out in the fields outnumbered the available ambulances by a hundred to one.

High on Ware's priority list was establishing a 'flying brigade' of private local cars and drivers who could assist the French in driving injured soldiers to field hospitals. Once a student in France, he spoke the language and was a good organiser. Within days he had cars and drivers working in a number of districts. As the wounded were plucked from the battlefields, Ware's attention began to shift to the bodies of the dead. It was impossible to bury them all so they often remained where they fell, their bodies unidentified except for their absence at the next roll call. The French picked up their own dead when they could but largely ignored the British and Commonwealth bodies. Considering them a health hazard, the corpses were occasionally set alight with whatever fuel was at hand, or dumped in mass pits. More often they were left to decay out in the open.

To reach a soldier crying out as he bled onto French soil, the cars travelling under the Red Cross flag sometimes were forced to drive over corpses lying scattered in the fields. Ware realised it was a case of priorities, however he also knew that every dead man or boy lying on those fields probably had parents or a wife and possibly children, waiting for their return; if they did not come back, their loved ones would want to know what had become of them. Having already sacrificed so much, they had a right to know and the only way to give them closure would be to identify the men who had given their lives and to bury them in a decent grave. It was an almost impossible task; to give a glimpse of the enormity of the problem, just one day of fighting in Mons had resulted in 35,000 deaths.

For the first time in history, the utter scale of the slaughter made the war casualties significantly visible. So many families were receiving messages that their men and boys had gone 'missing in action' that it was becoming an issue of major concern throughout the Commonwealth.

No one appeared to have responsibility for recording the ever-increasing numbers of bodies and maintaining the hasty graves left on the fields. There was no plan to mark these final resting places. So Ware set to work creating a record, identifying the dead, marking and recording the sites where they lay. Amid the bullets and the shells flying overhead, his dedicated team worked to save wounded men but also identified and secured bodies as they went.

In early 1915, taking matters into his own hands, Ware returned to England to explain to those in charge at the Imperial War Office that something must be done about the dead. Not only out of respect, although that was a high priority, but in view of health hazards, ethics and the demoralising effect all those strewn bodies were having on the soldiers.

Ware had discussed the idea of establishing an official organisation to perform the task of identifying and burying the dead with Lieutenant Colonel Edward Stewart, a Red Cross medical assessor. Stewart told him he had heard that the British authorities might not warm to Ware's idea of identifying the bodies on the front but instead might prefer to list the dead as 'missing', thus reducing the impact on public opinion.

If this was true then it was no more than a conspiracy of silence—a denial of their effort and a neglect of those men who had fallen. Ware wasn't a soldier and he wasn't a politician, but he had a hot evangelical zeal that surprised even himself at times. If needed he could be cold and methodical, but he was also tireless and a man with a cause who could work continuously for days on end. He would preach and talk until they understood. Returning to France without some kind of agreement was simply not an option.

In 1915, the War Office recognised Fabian Ware's work. In fact, his idea to create Graves Registration Units was met with applause. In March 1915, with the support of Nevil Macready, Adjutant-General of the British Expeditionary Force, Ware's work was given official recognition and support by the Imperial War Office and the unit was transferred to the British Army as the Graves Registration Commission. Brought under the command of the British Army, Ware's units were given official responsibility for finding, marking and registering Imperial graves in France. His work ultimately formed the basis for the Imperial War Graves Commission and by March 1915, Ware's Graves Registration Units were officially recording where British and Commonwealth soldiers were buried.

Ware was keen that the spirit of Imperial cooperation evident in the war was reflected in the work of his organisation. Encouraged by the Prince of Wales, he submitted a memorandum to the Imperial War Conference. In May 1917, the Imperial War Graves Commission was established by Royal Charter, with the Prince serving as president and Ware as vice-chairman.

It wasn't an easy job. If the men on Ware's unit were able to dig a decent grave, the sites situated in the area of a battlefront were often destroyed again by the frequent shelling of the same location. This would result in the loss of the original marked graves. On top of it all, the technical developments in the weaponry used by all sides frequently caused such dreadful injuries that it made the work of identifying or even finding a complete body for burial at times almost impossible.

On 11 November 1918, after four years of fierce warfare, three German government representatives accepted the Armistice terms presented to them by an Allied commander, General Foch of the French Army. It was five o'clock in the morning. The Armistice became effective at 11am the same day and, as the guns fell silent on the Western Front in France and Belgium, four years of hostilities at last ended. Worldwide more than 16 million people, soldiers and civilians, had lost their lives.

The unit received hundreds of requests from relatives for information or photographs of loved ones' graves. By the end of the war, some 587,000 graves in France alone had been identified and a further 559,000 casualties were registered as having no known grave. Ware's core belief was that none of the dead should be sent home. Every soldier of whatever rank, whether rich or poor, was to be buried in close proximity to where they had died. In Ware's vision, death was a democrat; upholding his beliefs, he prevented many wealthy families from retrieving their beloved dead. He envisioned a single nation—from all walks of life and all parts of the world—united in death, with every single grave, no matter the rank, identical to the next. The men were to be buried side by side, officers next to common soldiers.

Those who wanted to repatriate the bodies of their loved ones were refused permission. This refusal was often met with anger and resentment. The rule was not only an ethical decision, it was made on practical, economical and logistic grounds. Sending all those thousands of bodies home would have presented an enormous challenge.

To meet the demands of the public, the commission set the highest standards for all its work. Determined to ensure the ongoing recognition of the war dead beyond the conclusion of hostilities, three of the most eminent architects of the day—Sir Edwin Lutyens, Sir Herbert Baker and Sir Reginald Blomfield—were chosen to begin the work of designing and constructing the cemeteries and memorials. The famed author Rudyard Kipling was approached by Ware to act as literary advisor on inscriptions.

Kipling had lost his only son, seventeen-year-old John, during the battle of Loos in 1915. Due to his age, it had been difficult to get John into the army. Kipling, who, like Ware, was too old to serve, never saw a day's action and regretted it dearly, so he had urged his only son to go to the front. For weeks after hearing that John had gone missing, Kipling and his wife had done all they could to find a trace of him. They had written and spoken to people in high places, they had interviewed boys and men who had come back from the front, had visited field hospitals making inquiries. They never found him. Kipling knew first-hand how important it was for the bereaved to obtain some form of closure.

After the Armistice, the commission's work began in earnest. Once land for cemeteries and memorials had been guaranteed, the enormous task of recording the details of the dead began. And now the real work of recovering the dead could start. The magnitude of the task at hand became daunting even to the inexhaustible Fabian Ware, and the costs involved became outrageously expensive as the French earth surrendered one body after another. Ware called on all Imperial partners, especially Australia, to chip in and do their bit.

More than 50,000 Australian soldiers had perished on the Western Front in France and Belgium. The Australian Imperial Forces had established the Australian Graves Detachment with their own men working together with the British in France and Belgium. As the war had ended these Australian Imperial Force soldiers found themselves being demobilised quickly.

In October of 1919 the Australian Graves Detachment changed into the Australian Graves Services (AGS). Its men were recruited from those who were still serving with the Australian Imperial Forces. It was intended that the AGS would in time evolve from a military organisation into a civil one, mirroring its parent organisation, the Imperial War Graves Commission.

Poor leadership, mismanagement and financial abuse marked those first years in which the AGS was shaped. It was by no means a happy ship. With their headquarters across the Channel in London, the men, most of them coarsened and scarred by the war, were left behind in France and Belgium without proper guidance. Quarrels, insinuations, distrust and suspiciousness among the men led to an inquiry in France; after a grave turned up empty, accusations of hoaxing led to another inquiry in London.

This is the story of what happened.

Chapter 1
ROBERT DAVID BURNS
July 1916

On a fine morning on 20 July 1916, Lieutenant Robert David Burns died on a battlefield in France in what would come to be remembered as one of the saddest days in the Australian Imperial Forces history. The previous morning the men attached to his battalion had walked across the French countryside, passing pleasant cornfields and an occasional farmhouse. They were in high spirits, singing and joking as they made their way towards the front line.

They had disembarked almost three weeks before at Marseilles, having approached the French coast in beautifully clear weather. Those first views of the French coastline were rather pretty in comparison to the dry barren shores of Egypt, from where they had sailed.

Robert came from a family with a military tradition; his father was Colonel James Burns, former commander of the Australian 1st Light Horse Brigade, and his two older brothers were both in the Australian Imperial Force (AIF) and fighting on the front somewhere. Robert was the youngest of James's three sons. His first commission had been with the 4th Light Horse Brigade. After he had completed further training, on 27 January 1916 he was transferred to the 14th Australian Machine Gun Company attached to the 5th Division led by Major General James McCay.

Having fought a costly and unsuccessful campaign against the Turks at Gallipoli, the 14th Machine Gun was evacuated back to Egypt in December 1915. From the beginning of 1916 Australians were shipped to France. Robert had boarded the ship from Alexandria headed for France on 19 June. It was one of the last ships with Australian soldiers from Egypt heading for the French front.

From the window of the train that was now taking them to a small town just beyond Calais, the soldiers saw one river valley after another, all sprinkled with villages and farms. When they stopped at the stations, pretty girls with rosy cheeks came to welcome the foreign soldiers, giggling and blushing as they passed around sunflowers and cakes to the men. A handsome 27-year-old who rose to six feet five inches, Robert Burns was taller than most so he naturally got his fair share of attention from the ladies and he didn't mind one bit. It was nice to be noticed by these pretty girls after having seen nothing but the wrapped women of Egypt for months on end. As a soldier, he knew he must enjoy life while he could; the job he had chosen could very likely kill him. He had been lucky so far, however during his short but very intense service at Gallipoli he had witnessed what devastation the battlefield could bring and how randomly death could befall him or the men around him. So he winked at the rosy-cheeked girls who smiled back, blushed and blew an occasional kiss in return.

As the train pushed on, the country became flat and level and now French soldiers were appearing on the roads, waving as the engine driver saluted them by blowing the train's whistle. The stations and the kilometre-pegs were indicating that they were nearing Calais. Not very long afterwards they arrived at a little siding, which Robert later learned was Steenbecque; it marked the end of their long train trip from Marseilles. When they disembarked, they were instructed that their journey wasn't quite over and they would need to walk some miles to their camping place.

After receiving a rough sketch plan of the route and some rations, the men set off, but the map handed to them turned out to be quite confusing. After taking several wrong turns, the troop finally located their billets around midnight; a couple of local barns would serve as their sleeping quarters. Most of the men didn't mind—Egypt had turned out to be a bit of a culture shock for some, with no cafés in the sandy wasteland and almost no interaction possible with the locals. Many soldiers had felt alienated.

Here in France the countryside was green, girls had blown them kisses and given them flowers, and although they hadn't come across any yet, there were probably bars somewhere around where they might enjoy a cool beer. Who knows, there might even be a fish and chip shop in one of the small villages.

They could easily sleep in a barn in France. They had slept in far worse places, and they were dead tired after the long march and the straw floors appeared comfortable enough. Before Robert Burns fell asleep that night he became aware of the very distinct rumbling of mortar and realised they couldn't be far from the firing line.

The next morning, he found out they were about fifteen miles from the front and that they were scheduled to head for the battlefield very soon. Their commander had received news that his division would be among the first to go to the Fromelles–Aubers Ridge area. An earlier effort in 1915 to ward off the Germans there had failed and the idea now was to create a diversion by having the Australian 5th Division, together with the British 61st Division, engage with the enemy at Fromelles. This would draw the enemy's attention away from the Allies attack on the Somme and hopefully prevent the enemy from strengthening their forces there.

Their Australian commander, Major General James Whiteside McCay, was a former member of the Victorian parliament who had gone on to become a member of the first Australian federal parliament and subsequently served for two years as the young nation's minister for defence. Robert knew him as a down-to-earth soldier who did not very much appreciate fancy parade-ground movements or highly ornamented uniforms. Because he trained his men exhaustively, McCay was regarded by some as a bit of a tyrant. He also often brushed his fellow officers up the wrong way because of his tendency to regard all orders from the point of view of a lawyer and often to argue about them.

McCay's men, although they had been among the last to leave for Europe, would become the first to see serious action at Fromelles, a town close to France's northern border with Germany. They would be engaging in the first full-scale battle there and he expected much of them. After defeat at Gallipoli and the frustrations of Egypt, McCay was almost certain that his men would be prepared to put up a fierce fight.

The slaughter at Gallipoli had opened the eyes of the soldiers who had fought there to what a full-scale battle involved. However, McCay realised that although most of his men were well trained and had seen their share of fighting, many of them were also young and inexperienced; some had only had a week of training and some only one day. He wondered if they would be fully prepared for what was in store for them. The new arrivals had hardly enough time to get their bearings let alone prepare for action.

McCay had not discussed detailed battle plans with them as yet and some officers asked him how they were supposed to take over a sector without familiarising themselves with the setting. A few grumbling men were already complaining that they were being sent off to engage in a hastily arranged incursion that was doomed to fail.

The Battle of the Somme had begun almost three weeks earlier on 1 July 1916. British and French troops had attacked the enemy's deep defences near the Somme River, 19 miles from the city of Amiens, after an artillery bombardment that lasted a week. It was no secret that the British had suffered massive casualties on the first day. The Germans were as determined as the Allies and all anyone could do was hope that the effort on the Fromelles front would make a difference—that those men who would lose their lives in the coming battle would not lose them in vain. The thought that their taking part might help the Allies break though the enemy lines was a consolation to the soldiers.

What the Allies did not know was that the Germans knew they were coming and were ready and waiting for them. On 9 July, the British launched a diversionary operation in the direction of Fromelles and the Bare Ridge with the intention of destabilising the German front. On 16 July, an English bombardment had alerted the Germans that a massive attack might be launched within days. The 6th Bavarian Reserve Infantry Division, consisting mainly of recalled German reservists, gathered its troops together near Fromelles and placed them on maximum alert. The Allied attack had initially been planned for 17 July but was postponed until 19 July due to weather conditions.

It had rained almost continuously since the soldiers had left the train and a low mist hung in the shallow valleys surrounding the area. Without a visual there could be no attack. That evening McCay informed his men that their mobilisation to the front was postponed. A day later the weather improved and the fog that had shrouded the lowlands lifted and disappeared. The 5th Division finally received orders to head towards the front in the early morning hours of 19 July.

Walking through the French countryside, the men's laughter suddenly stopped as they entered a small village. It looked abandoned and the silence seemed to enhance the muted sounds of gunfire in the distance. To their left a large glass-roofed building had been destroyed, leaving only its walls still standing; inside was a mass of ruins and shards of glass. A little way up the road the contours of a church were visible but, as they neared it they noticed its steeple was full of holes and most of its main body had been shattered. The splintered timber of the building pointed towards the sky, almost in a gesture of anguish.

A group of young and inexperienced soldiers who had joined the 5th Division a few weeks previously had been hearing gunfire and mortar for a couple of days now, but up to this point they had not seen its effects. Walking through the small village they became quiet, witnessing destruction the likes of which they had never seen before. Some of them were barely sixteen years old, young boys lying about their age to sign up and thinking it an act of righteousness; proud fathers and worried mothers had waved them off as they left the shores of Australia. As the sound of artillery became louder and more distinct, they came to realise they might die in this foreign land.

In front of the church a statue had toppled over, probably because of an explosion nearby. It was a Madonna holding up a Christ child, the latter creating the shape of the cross with its outstretched arms. The Christ child was now leaning over, with one finger pointing towards the earth. A boy with the fear of God in him gasped and was not able to hold back his tears. He would not be the last one to cry—before the day was over, most of the younger boys would be screaming for their mothers.

As they marched on 19 July, the Germans had already positioned themselves on higher ground, well aware that a large division of Australians and British were approaching. They had brought in reinforcements and were patiently waiting for the enemy to arrive.

The sound of explosions was now very loud and in the distance the Australians could see soil spitting up into the air as bombs hit the earth's surface. There was no time to think about it. They came to an area where a protective wall consisting of timber and bags of earth had been built. The artillery fire muted the sound of their boots as they hit the wooden duckboards. Lee Enfield rifles were handed out to the newcomers. Gathered in a communication trench just before the front line, the men waited in anticipation as they finally received their instructions. Ready for combat, they secured their bayonets to their guns.

At Fromelles the opposing trench lines faced each other across a boggy, overgrown no-man's-land, through which ran a stream and a large number of muddy ditches. The constant rain had raised the water levels. The high water table made the trenches fill up with water, making it almost impossible to reach the frontline trenches.

At 11am the preliminary bombardment of the German zone began, but the Germans had expected it and taken precautions. Seven hours of intensive bombardment proved ineffective. A counter-bombardment from the enemy hit the front line of the Allies, effectively destroying their communication systems. Many men were dead or wounded before the actual attack had even begun.

At 6pm the assault signal finally came. Liberated from the stress of waiting, Robert and his men clambered out of the deep battlefront slit trench where they had sheltered and crossed the parapet, sprinting into no-man's-land without any cover. At first the sheer number of men running and screaming as they made their way across appeared to intimidate the enemy, and hardly a shot was fired. The soldiers running out into the open field did not know that the enemy had waited patiently for this moment. The Allies would have to cross 450 yards of open ground before they reached the German front line at a spot they called Sugar Loaf.

When the Germans opened fire, many men in Robert's battalion were cut down by enemy bullets before they were even halfway across no-man's-land. Robert himself had no time to stop and help as men fell to the ground around him. Trying to get his bearings, he jumped into a shell hole filled with murky water, hoping it might protect him for a moment; he only just managed to keep his machine gun from being soaked. Peeking above the lip of his makeshift trench, he caught a glimpse of the ruins of Fromelles village standing beyond the German forward lines.

The soldiers hiding in shallow trenches realised they had no alternative but to continue to descend upon the enemy lines, just as they had been ordered to do. Their orders were to gain and hold the trench on the German edge of no-man's-land. This appeared to be an almost impossible mission; even though the shelling was now becoming less ferocious, the men had still not managed to make it all the way to the designated trench.

A line of them fumbled with their machine guns as they dropped into a deep ditch, setting them up to face the enemy's next position. Robert had orders to hold these positions, but he realised that the Germans held the high ground with all its advantages. Their gunfire and shelling appeared to be coming from everywhere.

As the day wore on, corpses were left scattered across the fields in disarray, like raggedy puppets that had fallen from the sky. Thousands of men were slain by the enemies' artillery fire. Robert and what was left of his battalion were still out in the middle of no-man's-land, sheltering in a shallow ditch and desperately trying to hold the positions they had taken. Exhausted and dispirited, they shuddered in their soaked refuge as yet another German counterattack began. Any lingering thoughts of bravery or valour that some still might have fostered quickly evaporated as shells once again started exploding around them.

McCay's orders had been simple enough: they were to clear the enemy out of their trenches row by row. His exact words had been: 'The mode of taking out trenches should be as follows: first wave stays at and clears enemy out of first row of trenches. Then advance further. Second row passes first wave to next enemy row.'[1] Most men had memorised it and they were well aware what was expected of them, but now, as the enemy shellfire once again rained down, every man wondered how he was going to reach any German trench.

As Robert peered out, he could see Germans making their way towards the craters that speckled no-man's-land as a result of the previous bombing. Bellowing orders, he managed to re-energise his mortar and gun crews back to life. They would not die like rats in this ditch, at least not without putting up some kind of fight. Quickly realising they must stop the advance if they were to have any hope of surviving, the men took up their guns and spat bullets at anyone who tried to make his way towards them. Taking care not to hit any of their own soldiers, who were leaving their hiding places ready to thwart the advancing Germans with everything they had, they managed to stop the enemy's progress.

As the day wore on, the men felt sure they had done their work well. They had managed to ward off the German advance and now their enemy appeared just as tired as they were. The Allies could draw breath as the fierceness of the shelling around them abated.

Nevertheless, the fighting continued throughout the night with the German machine guns and other artillery spitting out shells and bullets at intervals in the direction of the occupied ditches and trenches. Bullets hissed by with a queer swishing sound, or cracked overhead with a noise like a stockwhip. Flares were constantly shot up in their direction from the German line, illuminating the desolate waste and outlining them as they huddled together, the light making them feel all the more vulnerable and exposed. The Australians did not know that the Germans were in the process of encircling them. In the end German grenades forced the men to leave their ditches, driving them out into the open.

In the early morning hours Australians and Bavarians found themselves fighting in close quarters, engaged in a man-to-man battle. As the soldiers ran out of ammunition they fought with their bayonets, knives or shovels, clubs or bare hands, anything to maim the enemy. This went on for five hours. By dawn the Australians were surrounded by the enemy on all sides and had lost hope. The order to retreat reached what was left of the troops around 6am, but they were encircled by the Germans and there was nowhere left to retreat to.

As the sun poked through the clouds, a young soldier who dared take a peek over the edge of the large ditch where a group of men sheltered got hit in the neck by a machine-gun bullet. A choking sound escaped from the boy's lips as Robert rushed down to him, taking a handkerchief from his pocket to bandage the wound. No one could do anything for him and the boy lay there for half an hour before he finally died. Afterwards Robert searched the body for the boy's identity disc and put it in his pocket, realising that some mother would want to know if and where her son had died. If he got out of this alive he would give the disc to the Red Cross and it would send it on to his parents.

By now the ditch was full of wounded and dying men groaning, crying and shrieking. 'Like a bloody butcher's shop,' someone whispered. Men were shouting to make themselves heard above the din and young frightened boys hugged whatever they could find, awaiting their fate. As soon as any of the men raised themselves above the ditches, they were shot back into it by German snipers. Most of the boys had stopped making any noise by now, shell-shocked into silence as their mates died around them. Robert realised they were trapped.

The enemy's relentless counterattacks pushed the Allied forces back, surrounding some groups and forcing others to fight their way back to their own lines, leaving their dead and wounded behind on the battlefield. As it became clear that the situation was hopeless, the Allies requested a conditional truce so as to gather and attend to the wounded who lay moaning in the open fields, but the Germans refused, knowing they would not benefit in any way from a truce. It was hell, the darkest hell Burns had ever witnessed. Hundreds of maimed men were scattered among the debris, hanging on barbed wire or sheltering in craters, their pitiful cries, clearly heard, growing thinner as death approached.

On the morning of 20 July, the 5th Division lost 5533 men in less than 24 hours and the British 61st Division, who had less men, lost 1547. Robert Burns was hit by a bullet on the morning of 20 July 1916. Loading his machine gun for the hundredth time, he suddenly found himself on his back looking up at the fresh blue sky as the rain ceased and the sun nudged over the sandbags on the rise of the trench. God, it was bright, he thought.

It was the last thought he would ever have.

Chapter 2
HOW IT CAME ABOUT
January 1919

In May 1917, the Imperial War Graves Commission (IWGC) was founded. While the organisation of its work was left to the British, all Commonwealth countries contributed financially to it and had a member on the commission's board. Andrew Fisher was appointed as Australia's first IWGC board member. He had previously served three separate terms as Prime Minister of Australia and was currently Australia's high commissioner to the United Kingdom.[1]

In September 1914 Fabian Ware had begun to record fatalities with his Red Cross unit and in March 1915 the unit was established as the Graves Registration Commission. It was incorporated into the British Army in October 1915. Graves Registration Units became responsible for recording the burial of the dead, but it was up to the military unit itself to carry out the actual burial. From October 1915, the English Graves Registration Commission had been officially recording where

Commonwealth soldiers were buried. Its role was to acquire land for the sole purpose of establishing cemeteries, to take care of the graves in such cemeteries, to complete and maintain records and registers of all men buried, and to erect memorials. Canadians, New Zealanders, South Africans, British and Australians were buried side by side in these cemeteries. The portion of the expenses that Australia was to contribute was £94,000 per annum, to be paid to the IWGC for six and a half years.[2] The Australian Imperial Forces in France established an Australian Graves Detachment (AGD). Many of those chosen to serve in the AGD were AIF men who had suffered injury or were deemed in some way unfit for other duty. This AIF detachment would help the English Graves Registration Units identify and bury the Australian bodies during the war.

In 1917 Australia's official war historian, Charles Bean, was the first to suggest a burial ground solely for Australians in France. Prime Minister Hughes stated that he was sure that the Australian government would be only too glad to do anything in its power to consecrate the last resting place of those fallen heroes, but the IWGC wasn't very keen on splitting up the commission into separate countries. As far as Fabian Ware was concerned, all soldiers from Commonwealth countries should be buried together, although as many as possible from a specific Commonwealth country should be laid side by side, creating a designated area within the cemetery. The Australians visiting France during those early years expected to find graveyards with only Australians buried in them. The reality was that all the Commonwealth soldiers were buried together. To help the bereaved who had made the long trip from Australia to Europe just after the war small signs were put up to let visitors know that 'Australians are also buried in this cemetery'.[3]

After the Armistice, it was estimated that some 160,000 corpses were still lying on the battlefields in northern France. Other bodies that had been buried in small, hastily established cemeteries, as bullets flew overhead, would need to be relocated. Soldiers buried in isolated graves would be exhumed and reinterred to a proper cemetery. But there were also thousands of invisible dead.

It was hard to find men who were willing to join the Graves Registration Units in the field after the Armistice. With peace, British soldiers scrambled to escape the horrific battlegrounds and so Ware was faced with a shortage of manpower. To recruit enough men for the ongoing work, an extra two shillings and six pence a week was added to their standard military pay. This helped and soon Ware's corps was at its desired capacity. To assist the British effort, at the beginning of 1919 Australia sent a thousand men from the AIF Australian Graves Detachment to help clear the area near Amiens. At the end of 1919, as the AIF started mass demobilisation of its men, this number diminished and the returning soldiers sometimes reported alarming stories about the many bodies still left exposed on French and Belgian soil.

During those first months of 1919 there were about five Australian graves units operating in different areas of France. The British maintained the task of exhuming the bodies, but the Australians were to identify them and remove any doubt about their nationality. After establishing the corpse's identity, the men working for the AGD were to reinter them in a decent grave in one of the designated cemeteries and mark the grave with a wooden cross until an appropriate headstone could be erected.

After the war had ended, recovering the dead became an important goal and the AGD was in need of thorough reorganisation. The task of registering the missing and dead, as well as the job of unearthing bodies, required a centralised and better organised agency. By the end of 1919 the soldiers working for the Australian Graves Detachment merged into the newly founded Australian Graves Services (AGS).

Most men recruited to the AGS were from the AIF, so the service was accountable to the military but also came under the administration of the high commissioner in London, Andrew Fisher. It was expected that over time the service would become a fully civilian one with its headquarters located at Australia House.

Australia House was a new major landmark in the city of London, standing at the end of The Strand and facing St Clement Danes Church at the top of Fleet Street. Due to shortages in Europe at the time, much of the material used in its construction was imported from Australia. Shipping problems caused by the war had delayed completion of the building, but on 3 August 1918 it had been officially opened. As the largest of all Australian overseas posts, it served the normal functions of embassy and accommodating the high commissioner, but it had a far wider range of activities than any other Australian embassy. In October 1919, it became the home to the Australian Graves Services.[4]

The first officer in command of the AGS was Quentin Shaddock Spedding, a Sydney-born journalist. At the age of eighteen Spedding had started work on the staff of *The Newcastle Morning Herald*; just a year later he became one of the founders of the Australian Journalists' Association. He later worked on the Sydney *Daily Telegraph* as its Melbourne representative. Like a lot of young men at the time, he wanted to do his bit and embarked for battle in May 1915.[5]

Spedding was one of the many who did not survive the war unscathed. A leg injury from an infected gunshot wound in France left him with a walking stick and a limp. Wounded in action on 16 March 1917, Spedding was taken from the front to one of the casualty clearing stations just behind the battleline. He was left on a stretcher outside a large tent where rows of wounded men were waiting for treatment. The clearing stations were the lifeline for the thousands of wounded and all the wards were constantly full. In operating theatres set up in tents, nurses and doctors worked around the clock to deal with the endless demand for amputations and other major surgery.

When a doctor came by to look at Spedding's wound, he inspected it with intense scrutiny. Without a word, the medic then left and went on to the next patient. Spedding thought nothing of it, but he later heard that the medic had suspected Spedding of inflicting the wound upon himself.

Self-inflicted wound patients were often treated with abhorrence by the hospital staff, occupying badly needed beds and demanding medical attention when others, who were considered more worthy, were waiting. Those believed to have committed this offence were subject to immediate arrest followed by a term of imprisonment.[6] An officer interrogated Spedding further. Luckily for him, some of the wounded soldiers in the ward were from his unit; they had been with him during the attack and vouched for him.

Unfit for battle duty, Spedding was detached from the Anzac Corps and returned to London to take up administrative duties. At the beginning of 1919 the AIF created the Australian Graves Detachment and Spedding became its liaison officer, dealing with the various burial authorities in France. By the end of July, Spedding, carrying the temporary rank of captain, was asked to become the officer in charge of the new Australian Graves Services.

At that time there were still many AIF men in France awaiting demobilisation. These men were asked to volunteer for the AGS and about 1000 of them did. They were sent to clear the land around the Fromelles and Pozieres battlegrounds of any bodies. They would stay employed by the AIF and enjoy additional benefits as they waited to be sent back to Australia. The work was tough, but the two issues of rum each day (the alcohol was thought to help kill dangerous germs that entered the body), as well as the extra money, made AGS jobs unusually popular.

Spedding's task was to create and organise units to finalise the work of establishing gravesites and reburying Australian bodies. Three towns were picked as a base for the Australian units: one unit in Villers-Bretonneux and one in Amiens—both very close to the Fromelles battlefield in northern France, where many Australians had perished—and one just over the border in Belgium at Poperinghe. Identification and reburial units were soon formed; to this were added an Australian photographic section as well as a memorial cross section. Until then, the British photographers working for the graves registration units had taken photos for the Australians on request. Both additional sections, as well as a motorised transport section based at Villers-Bretonneux, came under the command of one officer, Captain Charles Kingston.

In view of the fact that many relatives would want to visit the graves, it was thought that it would be a good idea to have Australian officials in the field in France. This work was to be coordinated by two centres, one at Amiens under Lieutenant William Lee and the other in Poperinghe under Major Alfred Allen. Alfred Allen would also be given the job of chief inspector of the Australian section in France and Belgium. Both officers were appointed at the same time, near the end of 1919, and both would also take charge of their own photographic, identification and motorised sections.

When Major Alfred Allen was appointed as chief inspector, Spedding objected to General Hobbs.[7] General Joseph John Talbot Hobbs was an architect. He was a small man, frail but full of energy and a keen sportsman, interested in fencing, gymnastics, rowing, sailing and boxing. He was also a devout Christian. In April 1918 Hobbs had been largely responsible for the recapture of Villers-Bretonneux and in January 1919 he was knighted and received the KCMG (Knight Commander of the Order of St Michael and St George). Hobbs became deeply involved in the erection of memorials to the Australian divisions, having been appointed to select sites, prepare designs and arrange for construction. Four of the five designs were his. Later he chose Polygon Wood for the memorial to the 5th Division and Villers-Bretonneux for the Australian national memorial.

Nonetheless, Spedding, however much he respected the general, thought he must oppose Hobbs's choice in the matter of Alfred Allen. The units in France were coming together nicely, Spedding told Hobbs, but he was not overjoyed at the idea that a person with little or no knowledge of military procedures was to administer such a responsible position. Spedding had not had a say in the matter, although his opinion had been sought in the appointment of Kingston and Lee. He was not keen on the fact that Allen hadn't come from the AIF, as was the general practice—he was a civilian. After speaking to Allen, Spedding had noticed that the man appeared to have no knowledge about the geography of France, nor any idea of the work that needed to be done. He let Hobbs know that this had surprised and worried him and, as a result, he could have little faith in Allen's capabilities as chief inspector.[8]

Hobbs quickly overruled Spedding's objection. Allen had been recommended to him by the English Red Cross, who spoke highly of him; he had worked for the Australian Red Cross throughout the war and held the honorary rank of major with them. Hobbs told him that Allen had, after he had been offered the job, joined the AIF and he would serve with the rank of captain.* He thought Allen would be a fine addition to

---

* In all files and testimonies Alfred Allen is always referred to as 'Major Allen'. I have maintained this usage throughout.

the Graves Services; like himself, the man had been a respected architect back in Sydney, an experience that could be valuable when it came to constructing memorials and establishing the layout of cemeteries, and also like himself, Allen was a man of faith. Spedding let it go at that, although he continued to distrust Allen's motives for joining the AIF.

Kingston, Lee and Allen had all received written instructions from Spedding concerning their tasks. But from the start Allen demonstrated a tendency to interfere in matters regarding the officers of the AGS. Spedding regarded the whole operation in France—all the suggestions as to what might be done and the schemes of operations planned, as well as the establishment laid down—as his to command. The units in place in France under the Australian Graves Services were organised and run by him and by no one else.[9]

During a meeting with Allen, Spedding clearly let him know that he would not accept any interference. Procedures laid out were his and he could boast that all his proposals had met the unanimous approval of General Hobbs, General Birdwood (who had been in charge of all Australian forces during the war), and the Australian prime minister and minister of defence, among others. He had not stepped up and applied as a candidate for officer in charge of the AGS; instead, he had been called across to England from France to discuss the position because he already had months of experience in that field of work with the AGD. So, when he was offered the job, he had naturally accepted.

When Allen came into the scheme of things, the organisation, as far as Spedding was concerned, was already well on its way to completion. While welcoming any useful suggestions, Spedding was not going to accept the harmful interference of someone who knew nothing of the work.

In an attempt to avoid any problems with the lines of authority, Spedding held a meeting and ordered his men not to interfere with one another and to confine themselves to their own specific tasks, reporting solely to Australia House. After the meeting Allen complained that the order from Spedding curtailed his powers as chief inspector. It would mean that if Allen witnessed any misconduct, he would not have any authority to intervene. He would also have no authority to change any procedures.

Lee was very unimpressed with Allen, whose rank especially appeared to aggravate him, and he let Spedding know how he felt. To Lee and some other members of his unit, the man was nothing more than a 'disguised civilian'[10] who constantly refused to introduce himself as Captain Allen but always presented himself as Major Allen. Lee himself was still only a lieutenant and Spedding could understand Lee's frustration. Allen had come in from the Red Cross, holding an honorary title. Spedding felt the same sense of dismay as Lee when Allen signed a document or introduced himself using his civilian rank of major. Hobbs explained that Allen could use the title if he wanted to; the title was never revoked and using it was not against any rule. Spedding secretly felt that if Allen could present himself as major then he himself, as the head of operations, should at least be granted the same status.

The establishment of the AGS was not getting off to a good start. Nonetheless, Spedding felt sure it was all due to start-up problems. Once everyone had settled in, matters would eventually sort themselves out.

Lee's complaints about Allen, however, were not the first time he had shown hostility towards a fellow officer. His relationship with Charlie Kingston was antagonistic at best. Lee disapproved of the way Kingston ran his unit; he told Spedding that Kingston could regularly be seen drinking and laughing with his men in French bars called estaminets and getting cosy with prostitutes.

In fact, complaints about slackness in France and other troubles had recently reached Spedding from various sources. One Ettie Rout had written a letter complaining about the Australian men's behaviour. Spedding had been introduced to Ettie Rout when he was in France. As far as he knew she was a New Zealander attached to the American Red Cross and she ran a soldiers' club.[11]

He was well aware that his men were a rowdy and tough lot. They had all been soldiers before coming to the AGS. They knew how to act as soldiers—how to fight, be brave and fearless. They also knew how to get drunk, chat up the ladies or find a prostitute, if only to forget, just for a moment, the horrors the war had presented. By joining the AGS, it was now expected that they would become clerks overnight.

Although Spedding had a doubt or two about some of the men, he was sure that all of them would in time realise how important their responsibility as members of the unit was, locating and burying their comrades. Spedding also understood that it was new terrain for almost every man on the unit and everyone was still getting their bearings. Adjusting would take time; it was a learning curve for all of them.

Based in London, Spedding relied on his officers in France to be his eyes and ears in the field, but he tried to cross the Channel twice a month to speak to Lee, Kingston and Allen personally. During one of those visits, Lee had approached Spedding with a number of complaints about Kingston. Spedding thought that Lee's allegations were so insistent that they took on the appearance of a private vendetta. Spedding promised Lee he would look into things the next time he popped over to France, but he hoped he wouldn't have to address Kingston. He felt certain everyone would settle down in due time.

It was around the beginning of his AGS appointment that Spedding received a letter from the Australian Red Cross.[12] They wanted information about the location of the body of a Lieutenant Robert Burns, whose family was looking for him. Spedding's office was receiving ever more requests from families seeking information about the whereabouts of their loved ones. He asked one of his staff, Sam MacMillan, to send this letter off to Alfred Allen to give him something to do. Spedding thought it might prove just how adequately fit Major Allen was for the task at hand.

Chapter 3
WILLIAM LEE

If you asked Billy Lee outright, he would without hesitation acknowledge that he thoroughly despised Allen Charles Waters Kingston. Kingston had irritating ways about him and was especially derogatory towards Lee. Billy certainly wasn't going to be made a fool of now that he had become an officer—least of all by 'Charlie the Boozer' or 'Bastard', as Kingston was commonly known to his men.[1]

Billy Lee, although still a lieutenant, felt he had earned himself some status now as assistant inspector in France. If Charlie thought he could put one over him then he had another thing coming.

Lee was just under six foot with a dark complexion, grey eyes and brown hair. He had worked the mines in Queensland but also claimed to have fifteen years' experience in the railways and electrical works. Although just over 40 years of age when he enlisted in the AIF in 1915, the army had welcomed him.[2]

A year later, in 1916, he was fighting in France. After the Armistice, he didn't much care to return to Australia.

He had sent a letter to the AIF asking not to be demobilised or discharged until the end of 1919, the reason being that his wife and his brother would be coming over to England in late October and the three of them would then proceed on to Nigeria. The plan was that Lee and his brother were going to follow their calling to set up a mining company in Africa.[3] Whether this was wishful thinking on Lee's part or not, he was so keen on staying that he literally begged the AIF for an appointment somewhere in Europe.

The army had its advantages. The pay was good and regular, and back home the only one waiting for him was Althea Beatrice—his wife, Bea. Lee wasn't a Casanova by any means, but here in France he had been able to enjoy the 'friendliness' of the French women and had acquired a taste for it. He'd even found himself a girlfriend of sorts. France was where he wanted to be for the time being, and he didn't feel a great need to go back to Bea.

At this time, the world was still picking up the pieces of the past four years and it took more than six months before an actual peace treaty was signed. The Treaty of Versailles, signed on the 28 June 1919, finally and officially brought World War I to an end. It had taken months of Allied negotiations at the Paris Peace Conference to conclude the treaty.

Wanting to stretch his stay in France, Lee had heard rumours that a new unit called the Australian Graves Services was going to be formed. Lee volunteered and, much to his own surprise, he was taken on for the job; not only that, but he was also given the job of assistant inspector of the AGS. His surprise at being offered this job stemmed from an accusation filed against him just one year prior. He claimed he had accidentally made an error in payments to his men, awarding himself some twenty pounds that he had not been entitled to. The small inquiry into the matter did not actually prove that this had been an accident and Lee was reprimanded by the AIF and even put on temporary suspension. Australia House and the AGS did not appear to know about it, and Lee was certainly not going to enlighten them.[4]

Lee was selected as assistant inspector of the AGS in France around the same time that a man named Adolf Hitler gave his first speech for the German Workers' Party. The AIF Graves Detachment had previously worked in conjunction with Fabian Ware's Imperial War Graves Commission and had consisted of about 800 to 900 men, split into five companies and given different areas in northern France to help locate the bodies of Australian soldiers. The AGS was to carry on this work, but the number of men employed by the new unit would gradually be reduced.

Before he was sent to Amiens, Lee was put in charge of a company of about two hundred men who were to operate in the region of Villers-Bretonneux, a small town that had been severely battered during the war. It had been the scene of two consecutive shattering confrontations.

The Germans had been very keen to capture the town because of its close proximity to the city of Amiens and its strategically important road and rail junction. Capturing this seemingly trivial landmark would have brought the Germans within artillery range of their enemy as well as Amiens. In late March 1918, Australian troops were brought in from Belgium as reinforcements to help defend the line and in early April the Germans launched an attack to capture Villers-Bretonneux, but the determined Australian and British troops managed to halt the German advance.

During a second battle at the end of April the Germans bombarded the area behind the town with mustard gas, causing a thousand Australians to perish. Afterwards Villers-Bretonneux fell into the hands of the enemy and, while still some distance from Amiens, the Germans now posed a clear threat to the city. If in the next step of their advance they could capture the hill overlooking Amiens, they would be able to bring down accurate fire on the town and seize their target. It became vital for the Allies to swiftly retake Villers-Bretonneux.

The Allies managed to do just that, following the first tank-versus-tank battle in history. The fields south of Villers-Bretonneux became the location of a duel between three British tanks and three German ones. One German tank was knocked out by the British and abandoned, and not much later the other German tanks retreated. Two Australian brigades and two British ones were then rushed forward to retake the town. By late morning, when the British–Australian attack commenced, the Germans who had not escaped were trapped in the town. By the time Villers-Bretonneux had been retaken, Australian casualties were more than 2400 but the German loss, including prisoners taken when the town was surrounded, was about

10,000. It was now the task of Lee and his unit to find the slain Australian men, identify them and rebury them in proper cemeteries.

Lee realised he'd been appointed mainly because of his age but, never having been anything but a private in the army, the responsibility and the job of assistant inspector that came with it made him feel important and he took the job very seriously. He received his instructions from Captain Quentin Spedding in London.

As the registration staff officer for the AGS at Australia House, it was Spedding who had been responsible for appointing Lee as assistant inspector of the area. Between August and September, the system had changed and the great bulk of the men were repatriated, leaving only a relatively small group in France to do the work. Lee was allotted some staff: Sergeant Black, Sergeant Coughlan and a personal driver called Edwards. He had never had any staff and never anything as magnificent as a personal driver. Being the head of this small unit gave Lee a sense of power and importance.

The whole procedure of recovering and identifying so many dead bodies was new for the men who had recently volunteered for the job. As before, the English would be in charge of digging up the bodies because they already had quite a lot of experience in the field, and the Australian Graves Services would be responsible for identifying and reburying their own people. While the officers in France were waiting for developments from London, they started rigging up their own administrative system, based on what the English already had.

After Lee got his orders from Australia House he went to work. He was determined to make a success of his position and, although he took to the task at hand with almost solemn dedication, it turned out to be a very complicated and demanding job. At times Lee and the men on his unit would become weary and disheartened by the work. It was dirty and time-consuming, and dealing with the state of the excavated bodies was a gruesome task. Heavy rain could turn the landscape into a sea of mud and by October temperatures had dropped and it became very cold.

There was never any lack of bodies though. Lee and his men came across corpses lying in fields all over the region's countryside. After the British exhumed a body and it had been recognised as Australian, Lee's men were to transport what was left of it to a permanent gravesite. That was the relatively simple part of the job; the hard part was undoubtedly identification.

During battle, dead mates were hastily buried in shallow graves; but later those graves were sometimes exposed to shelling and destroyed, leaving body parts scattered around. In this situation identifying a body was almost impossible. It was very difficult when a body was found in one piece but there were no tags or other items present. Soldiers on the battlefield would sometimes pocket the identification tag from the body of one of their fallen mates, intending to give the tag to the Red Cross or send it to the soldier's family. But if they in turn were killed, their bodies would be found carrying two identification tags and it would become a puzzle for the AGS men to find out the true identity of the corpse. The men would at times need to grope around in the body's remains, searching for a cigarette box, a letter, something that would confirm who they had found.

Lee, having been a manual labourer all his life, found the administrative part of his job quite stressful—recording and registering the dead along with all the other organisational work. His responsibilities at times became almost too much for him to bear. The stress of this situation intensified the animosity between Charlie Kingston and himself.

Lee knew the type of man Charlie Kingston represented. He'd seen his like before—fellows who were popular with the men but of dubious character and probably popular because of this trait. Lee was well aware that most AGS men were of good character, but he also recognised a larrikin when he saw one. He'd come across a few during his time in the army—inner-city boys, most of them, and a few of them had been shipped off to war after having been sentenced for some crime or another. Not that he knew of Kingston being involved in any wrong-doings before the war but Lee felt the man did not show the responsibility that went with the job.

For Lee it became evident that all his problems had begun when Charles Kingston was based in Villers-Bretonneux, taking over 'his' battalion headquarters in the town's chateau. Kingston was sent to replace Lee, so that Lee could move on to Amiens. Lee knew Amiens was a better place to be. Those living in the midst of the civilisation of Amiens and Poperinghe were able to enjoy the comforts of a hotel and the social distractions that any town offers, whereas the men at Villers-Bretonneux, living on the edge of the ruined town, were obliged to spend their lives in the shattered remains of a once magnificent chateau.[5] But Lee could not leave right away, because he had to instruct Kingston on the ins and outs of procedures at Villers-Bretonneux.

Lee didn't take to Kingston from the start; they were clearly opposites. Kingston was young and brash; he liked a drink and was chummy with his men. He didn't act like an officer, Lee thought. It became obvious to the men that the older Lee and the younger Kingston did not appreciate each other's company. But they did not have to put up with each other for very long because, just two months after Kingston arrived, Lee left for Amiens. Lee felt he had completed a thorough handover.

—■—

During the war, little had been done in the way of permanent grave works, but when Lee was stationed at Villers-Bretonneux he had managed to establish three cemeteries in and near the town. It had not been easy to correct errors made during the process of hasty burials throughout the war. Sometimes the men in the AGS would even stumble upon multiple graves in the field bearing the same name. Lee came across faults in the spelling on crosses or names that had become impossible to read because weather conditions had almost wiped them from the surface of the hastily erected wooden crosses.

A typed list of duties had been sent to him from Australia House, but unfortunately the 'Notes for the guidance of Inspectors and Staff'[6] did not offer any solution for when the records showed that one body appeared to be buried in two positions. Lee was forced to improvise and deal with problems as they arose and he felt that, so far, he had done so admirably.

Inquiries about the whereabouts of missing soldiers had been arriving from Australia House daily when he was working at Villers-Bretonneux. With the war ended for months now, quite a few people were realising that their loved ones, who had not been listed as killed in action, were not returning home. Some hoped that their sons or husbands were shell-shocked and still hospitalised, or feared they were roaming the French countryside, too traumatised to remember who they were. Families almost lost hope as time wore on, but with a responsible party now at hand, they turned to the AGS, seeking answers.

As one man after another was reported missing by their family in Australia, the bereaved demanded to know if their loved ones had been found, dead or alive, and if not, why not. When could they expect an answer and would it be of any use if they came over to France to search the countryside themselves? The letters were often sent to the Red Cross who would send them on to the AGS. They in turn would ask the AIF to look into their files and try to find out in which area the listed men had been fighting. If a suspected location could be found for the missing soldier then the AIF sent the location back to the AGS, who would send it to the men in the field to look into. Lee handled request after request.[7]

After Lee left Villers-Bretonneux, he did not take all his belongings from his quarters there. Setting up a unit in Amiens took time and Lee had busied himself with the preliminary work and left furnishing his new billet to a later date. When he finally did come back to Villers-Bretonneux to pick up his belongings, he found his former billet cleared out and all his things gone. His small library, his gramophone and his army kit, blankets and such—all gone.

Initially his main suspect was, of course, Charlie Kingston. Marching into Kingston's office, Lee confronted him, but Kingston denied any blame and made it clear to Lee that he had nothing to do with it. Kingston told Lee to go ask Ettie Rout about it. She had most likely taken Lee's stuff.[8]

Although Lee felt that Kingston was the culprit, he could also believe that Rout had something to do with the missing items. Lee had already experienced run-ins with the notorious Ms Rout. She had previously complained about the behaviour of the AIF personnel in France, specifically naming Lee and Kingston, and had sent a letter to the AIF to let them know that she found their behaviour intolerable.[9] She had also gone to the press.

Lee and Kingston had been so upset by Rout's accusations that they had demanded she either apologise to them publicly or be court-martialled for her conduct. It was one of the only topics they appeared to agree about. They drew up a petition voicing their complaints and it was signed by a number of officers, but it did not come to anything. Rout, although born in Australia, was working for the New Zealand and American Red Cross; she had become a New Zealand national and was out of reach of Australian jurisdiction.

Lee thought Rout's accusations of bad conduct might be right when it came to Kingston and his men, but he did not think she had any right at all to complain about him. For Lee, it was Ettie Rout who should be under scrutiny. He claimed she was the one running a dubious soldiers' club on Red Cross money.[10]

Rout had come from New Zealand and arrived in Villers-Bretonneux in 1919. She ran a depot funded by the American Red Cross, but she played up her Australian origins, well aware that the Australians were popular in the area. They were considered heroes by the French after the recapture of Villers-Bretonneux. The town's old school building had been rebuilt with money raised by Australian schoolchildren and Australian soldiers had helped with the construction; as a token of appreciation, every blackboard in the school carried the inscription *N'oublions jamais l'Australie* (Let us never forget Australia). Ms Rout, as she was commonly known, would often let herself be photographed with groups of AIF men. She cooked for the children in the area and took care of the pregnant women.

Rout also operated her depot as both a hotel and a soldiers' club. Accommodation was always free and she charged just a few pennies for a meal. She wrote many articles and sent them off to newspapers; most of them were about her particular disgust with New Zealand for not sending over any men to bury their dead. Articles appeared in the New Zealand newspapers in 1919 and aroused public awareness of the plight of the families who wanted a resting place for their loved ones.[11]

She was also in the business of trying to prevent venereal disease. Not much had been done during the war to avoid syphilis and gonorrhoea and, as a result, VD had spread like mildew among the soldiers. During the war Rout had acquired an infamous reputation as a fervent safe-sex campaigner. Wanting to see VD treated as a medical problem, not a moral one, she had become a great promoter of methods to prevent sexually-transmitted diseases.

Rout, adamant that something needed to be done about the soldiers becoming ill, discovered that the Germans, unlike the Imperial soldiers, had received prophylactic kits during the war. Curious about the compounds that they were using, she visited some German soldiers still held in French POW camps. They showed her the suppositories that they were to hand over to the women they slept with, which were intended to ward off disease. Rout tried out the kit on herself but found the compounds 'more or less unsatisfactory', because they made her feel ill. Inquiring among the foremost doctors in this new field, she combined the work of several to produce a prophylactic kit containing calomel ointment, condoms and Condy's crystals (potassium permanganate).

Rout urged the soldiers to visit Madame Yvonne's brothel if they were looking for a woman. Madame Yvonne had agreed to run her brothel on 'safe sex' lines and Rout inspected it regularly. Later, other brothels opened their doors to her and by the end of 1919 quite a number of brothels in Villers-Bretonneux were meeting the hygiene and safety standards Rout had imposed. She also encouraged women to take good care of their bodies and to take responsibility for their own sexual health.

All this made her a highly controversial figure. Her intense interest in the sex lives of the soldiers did not win her any popularity points with the military, who believed she was advocating irresponsible behaviour. They believed in discouraging any dealings whatsoever between the soldiers and women of ill repute. The men themselves were indignant that a woman was interfering in their private lives, and they accused her of putting her nose in where it didn't belong.

Lee did not think highly of Ms Rout and claimed that she ran a disreputable soldiers' club in her hotel. Lee had declared the hotel and the club 'out of bounds' to his men. He doubted that the Australian Red Cross had any knowledge of Ms Rout.[12] This was an accusation that Rout did not deny—she was working not for the Australian Red Cross but for the American and New Zealand branches.

When Lee confronted her about the loss of his personal possessions and the possibility that she might have had something to do with it, she reacted with disgust. He reported all this, of course, as well as his suspicions and Kingston's allegations. A few weeks later he got some of his belongings back anonymously through Australia House. However, a large number of items, worth about 30 pounds, remained lost.

Lee first met Major Allen in Amiens when he came down from Poperinghe to inspect and hold a meeting there. They immediately got off on the wrong foot when Allen took on an air of authority and demanded to inspect Lee's books. Lee denied him any access. Due to the somewhat vague orders from Australia House, Lee assumed that he himself was in charge of matters in France and that Allen only had authority in Belgium.

Lee had been given to understand that he was to deal with Australia House and Captain Spedding directly, so he felt in no way answerable to Allen.[13]

Villers-Bretonneux was just ten miles up the road from Amiens and Lee needed to drive there regularly to pick up supplies. Kingston was now in charge of the transport and photographic sections at Villers-Bretonneux and with each visit Lee's disgust at the way the camp was run intensified. At some point Lee became so annoyed that he committed his strong feelings to paper and sent it to the Australian Graves Services in London but received no reply. Frustrated by the lack of response from London, Lee, although not altogether thrilled with the new major in Belgium, turned to Allen. He asked him to have a talk with Kingston, especially about the way he was running his unit. Lee hoped that, because of Allen's higher rank, he might be able to talk Kingston around.

Lee let Allen know that one matter was especially frustrating to him: collecting his pay. Kingston was responsible for paying all the men and on Saturday he would go to a field cashier to draw the money. He chose to pay the men in one of the estaminets in Amiens; this, for Kingston, was the most convenient and logical place to do so. Most of the soldiers would gather there on payday for a drink and a chat, and he could pay them all without having to visit each of them separately.

Lee, however, refused to go to an estaminet to collect his salary. Although he was a regular visitor there, Lee thought an estaminet an inappropriate place to collect his money. Lee wanted Kingston to come by and pay him in his office in

Amiens. It had to do with respect from a young officer towards an older one.

The problems between the two men escalated when on pay-day Kingston passed Lee's office as he headed back to Villers-Bretonneux, refusing to stop by to pay him. This meant that Lee would have to go to Villers-Bretonneux to get his money or accept a delay in pay. It left the older man feeling terribly slighted and humiliated by the younger man. Lee saw it as a deliberate attempt to embarrass him in front of his men.

When Spedding visited Amiens, Lee vented his anger to the senior officer. Although Spedding listened sympathetically to his complaints, Lee did not feel confident that he would do much about it. Spedding did not seem eager to confront Kingston and appeared willing to wait, thinking the whole matter might blow over. It was all right for him, Lee thought—Spedding was comfortably far away in London and only came over every now and again.

When Lee next had a meeting with Alfred Allen he had hoped for a willing ear, but he was once again disappointed by the reaction he got. Allen responded aloofly and told him he would look into the matter in due time. So Lee, tired of being brushed off, threatened Allen that he would go to the AIF and demand an inquiry into the shameful misbehaviour of Kingston and his men.

At this Allen almost laughed out loud.[14] He explained to Lee that his chance of ever being granted an inquiry was probably naught. He also told him: 'You have always got troubles. Can't you try to get on better with Captain Kingston?' But Lee said that as far as he was concerned, this would be impossible. All he wanted was for Allen to take up the matter of the pay arrangements with Kingston, but he didn't.

On top of all this, Lee got word that Kingston had been mouthing off about him. One of the new clerks at Amiens, Costin, told him that Kingston had said that Lee was unfit for the job he had been given, that he had made a mess of things and that his wife was requesting the AIF to provide information on his whereabouts. She was asking them to demobilise him and send him back to Australia when they had located him.

Lee had an inkling as to where that rumour had come from and he told Costin that it was all a blatant lie. Other small rumours found their way to him, making him feel uneasy. He felt that everyone was against him and he had no one to talk to. He also felt they were 'trying to squeeze him out of the place'.[15]

Stressed by the job, fed up with the situation with Kingston and with no outlet to vent his anger through, Billy Lee, having served just a few months with the newly formed AGS, decided to go to war over the matter.

Chapter 4

ALLEN CHARLES WATERS KINGSTON

Charlie Kingston was only 23 years old when he joined the AIF in 1914.[1] He probably detested Billy Lee just as much as Lee did him. He thought Lee's habits left much to be desired: the man was not only ugly but he also had hygiene issues. In Kingston's view he was also just plain dumb, and Kingston could not understand how such a dimwit had managed to secure the job of assistant inspector.

Allen Charles Waters Kingston had been a farmhand before the war, so he was not exactly a scholar either, but Lee was as thick as his mum's socks and crabby to boot. Always complaining about Kingston drinking with his men in the estaminets, as if Lee didn't drink, and ordering Kingston to pay him his salary in his office. Who did he think he was? He was just a pretentious nobody. Or so Kingston and quite a few of his men thought.

Kingston found some pleasure in getting the man aggravated and had on one occasion driven past Lee's office on his way back to Villers-Bretonneux without stopping, driving slowly to make sure that Lee had seen him. He just couldn't understand why Lee wouldn't come to the bar like everyone else to collect his pay; he suspected Lee's demand to pay him in his own office was a way to underline the notion Lee had that he was the older and the wiser officer. To Lee, Kingston was just a snotty kid. Charlie knew he might be a snotty kid, but he was in charge of the money.

Kingston had not been a bad soldier; in fact, his bravery in battle had not gone unnoticed. During the war, he had fought under Colonel Stan Perry with the 45th Battalion as part of the transport section. Colonel Perry, a chemical engineer, had held the line at Fleurbaix and then on the Somme in 1916 where he was severely wounded in battle near Pozières in August. Perry did not make a fuss of it and, despite his serious injuries, he was back on the front ready to lead his men by December. During the battle to break the Hindenburg Line in 1918, it was Perry who noticed that Kingston, who was a driver, had acted quite courageously throughout. Heavy daytime shelling had never stopped him doing his duty; as a transport driver, he would rush in with supplies and ammunition. At night, despite heavy bombing, Kingston had put his own life at grave risk repeatedly as he supplied the soldiers in the trenches. In the aftermath of the battle Perry had seen fit to have him awarded the Distinguished Conduct Medal for 'distinguished, gallant and good conduct in the field'.[2]

After the Armistice, Kingston became a transport officer for the AIF's Australian Graves Detachment. He had been present when the people of destroyed French villages and towns slowly began to return home. When the Australians managed to liberate Villers-Bretonneux from the Germans in July 1918, the townspeople had been eager to show their gratitude for the Australian sacrifice. Kingston was delighted that his post was at this town when the Australian Graves Detachment became the Australian Graves Services and he was appointed officer in charge of the transport and photographic units.

—■—

Kingston knew all about cars, but he knew nothing about photography. Taking pictures with a camera had taken off during World War I; it was the first conflict ever to be photographed in detail. By the time the war broke out in 1914, all the skills and technical resources to take photographs under the most difficult circumstances possible were already in place. Using smaller cameras and film formats, it became easy for professional photographers to make images quickly and under difficult light conditions. A little Kodak camera called the Vest Pocket was the most popular camera carried by soldiers. Although forbidden by some militaries, including Britain, because of the danger that photos could supply the enemy with valuable information, many soldiers inadvertently or not took cameras to the front.

Sent to the front in August 1917 with the honorary rank of captain, Frank Hurley became Australia's first official war photographer.[3] James Francis Hurley was then 27 years old and already well known in Australia for his work. He was no stranger to making images under risky conditions.

Just three years earlier, in 1914, he had joined Ernest Shackleton's expedition to Antarctica where their ship, the *Endurance*, became stranded on pack ice. Marooned for months, the crew watched their only means of escape, their ship, slowly being crushed by ice. Barely able to survive and feeding themselves by eating their dogs, Shackleton's men were forced to drift on great slabs of ice for more than a year. Despite this desperate struggle for survival, Hurley had managed to produce a stunning set of images.

Again risking life and limb, he set to work on the Western Front to document the conflict taking place. Influenced by what he had read in newspapers—articles about the great courage of the Australian soldiers on the battlefields—Hurley had expected to be able to shoot glorious and uplifting images. But what he saw appalled him. In his diary he wrote: 'One dares not venture off the duckboard or he will surely become bogged, or sink in the quicksand-like slime of rain-filled shell craters. Add to this frightful walking a harassing shellfire and soaking to the skin, and you curse the day that you were induced to put foot on this polluted damned ground.'[4]

Because of the risks he would take to secure a photograph, the soldiers dubbed him 'The Mad Photographer'. Hurley did not have many friends. His behaviour and his often crude way of communicating brushed people up the wrong way, but the man was a warrior with a camera and prepared to venture anywhere and do anything to get a picture.

Trying to capture the reality of battle close-up, Hurley needed light, but anyone stepping onto the parapet of a frontline trench in daylight was likely to be shot dead by a sniper within seconds. Not being able to produce the images he wanted, he began to manipulate his war pictures by combining visual elements from separate photographs, merging them into a single image, thus creating the illusion that all those elements were part of the same scene. In his role Hurley was under the formal command of historian Charles Bean, with whom he had a difficult relationship. A particular quarrel with Bean—who did not much like Hurley's photography, which he labelled as 'fake'—escalated when Bean got General Headquarters to prohibit Hurley from making composites. Bean thought this way of presenting the battlefield was misleading. Hurley's composites were a false display of events and the historian did not think Hurley's 'fake' photographs should be shown to the public.

Hurley, utterly disgusted with Beans accusations, considered sending in his resignation and took his case to the chief of the Australian forces, General Birdwood, who negotiated a compromise. In return for withdrawing his resignation, Hurley was allowed to contribute six composites to a London exhibition devoted to Australia's fighting in France. These exhibited images made their way into the Australian newspapers and finally the public could see what their sons and husbands were enduring. Those eerie images were the first real war photos to reach Australia, and the startlingly beautiful, but also horrifyingly gruesome, images brought home to the common Australian what the war looked like up close.

There were eleven photographers serving at Villers-Bretonneux and their task was to take a photograph of every Australian grave that was discovered. Most of Kingston's men were certainly not Frank Hurleys in the making; they were not even remotely professional photographers. As long as they could hold a camera and knew the basics, they would be taken on by the AGS. Professional photographers were hard if not impossible to come by, and with so many men returning home this was not a time to be picky. So the AGS employed men from all walks of life to serve in the photographic section. How hard could it be, anyway, to take a picture? There was an overwhelming demand from relatives in Australia for photos. With no actual grave at home to mourn over, the prints provided a much needed substitute shrine for the bereaved.

The self-taught unit set out daily to supply Australia House with images of individual graves. For these amateurs, however, the actual developing of their film was a different thing altogether. At a loss as to how to go about this, the photographic unit sent their film directly from France to England; the photographic section at Australia House would develop, print and distribute the photos from London.[5] This almost always presented problems, because the results from developing the film weren't exactly a cause for great enthusiasm—they were often a series of grainy black-and-white images with the actual words on the crosses of graves marred by bad lighting or incompetent photography. Errors inevitably crept into the photos. People who were present in the graveyard when the photographs were taken sometimes unintentionally showed up in the background. A Chinese stonemason appeared behind a tomb after one of the negatives was printed and a German prisoner sleeping near a post also emerged unexpectedly in a photo. So a request would have to be sent to France for a photograph to be taken again.[6] Everyone agreed it was a time-consuming and inefficient process. However, if the developed film was deemed good enough, three prints would be made of each negative and those would be forwarded to the next of kin free of charge.

It was the photographic staff's job to systematically document the cemeteries. In good weather, a photographer was expected to obtain some fifty usable pictures a day, but Kingston's men rarely met this brief. Kingston claimed that this wasn't due to any laziness on the part of his men but more often by weather conditions and lack of mobility. Cars were scarce and often undergoing maintenance.

During those first months Kingston had only one car to transport his photographers to and from the cemeteries. Although there had been more cars when Kingston started at Villers-Bretonneux, they had either broken down, been left in the field and dismantled, or had just simply disappeared. The one car they still had was also used to transport rations and it was frequently in repairs. Left without transport, the photographers sometimes had to walk twenty miles in order to carry out their duties. By October it was winter and, with weather conditions deteriorating, the men complained that the failing light made photography almost impossible.

—■—

Chateau Delacour, where Kingston's men were lodged on the outskirts of the town, had been rechristened the 'Red Chateau' by the Australian forces because of its red brickwork. During the Battle of the Somme it had served as headquarters and billets for Allied generals and at the end of the hostilities in November 1918 it became the local headquarters of the Imperial War Graves Commission. Now it was home to the transport and photographic sections of the AGS.

Up until the end of 1919 Kingston and his men were living in the chateau and some factory buildings on the grounds, but by the end of December the owner of the property, Madame Henriette Delacour, told them they would need to seek other accommodation. She wanted her buildings back. It came as a shock to Kingston and he arranged a meeting with Madame Delacour in an effort to convince her to let them stay. After some persuasion, Delacour gave the Australians permission to remain on the chateau's grounds, but they could no longer stay in the main house. They would have to erect their own huts on the grounds, she decided, but they could stay there without paying rent. So all through the bitterly cold Christmas and New Year, the men collected materials to build shelters. Makeshift barracks slowly arose on the chateau's grounds, the small wooden structures resembling an assortment of rural sheds.

From the start Kingston complained about the organisation of Australian Graves Services, which he described as at least 'faulty'.[7] Lee was in charge of Amiens, he himself was in charge of Villers-Bretonneux and in mid-1919 one Major Alfred Allen was introduced to both of them as inspector for the Poperinghe area just over the Belgian border. Kingston assumed that both he and Lee would now be answerable to the new major, but

Spedding told them that Allen's official rank was captain and that they were to report individually to Australia House in London. Spedding had made it clear that the three of them were to meet once or twice a month to discuss problems and progress, but that none of them had any authority over the other.

It also became clear to both Lee and Kingston that the new officer was not AIF like the rest of them. Kingston didn't know what to think of the man, who on first meeting introduced himself as Major Allen. He had other reservations, mostly due to the fact that Allen had not really served in the army in any capacity; still, he appeared to have some knowledge of administrative work. At this time Kingston did not have anything against Allen and he tried to be as helpful as he could when Allen sought his help.

However, this changed when, at the end of December, Allen approached Kingston to let him know that he thought all of the work should go through him. This surprised Kingston very much because he had heard nothing that suggested such an arrangement from Australia House. Kingston let Allen know that he would wait for instructions from either Spedding or anyone else from Australia House first. When no word came from London, Kingston assumed that Allen had not pursued the matter and he left it at that.[8]

Due to the animosity between Kingston and Lee, all communication between them was conducted through Allen. When they came together during the fortnightly meetings, Kingston and Lee refused to speak with each other. Kingston was well aware that Lee had complained about him to the major because Allen had taken him aside and informed him of as much. Allen asked Kingston if there was any truth in the complaints Lee had made. Kingston replied that Lee was always causing trouble; he seemed to have quarrels with everyone and Kingston had no idea why Lee was being so difficult.

Allen had heard from Lee that Kingston drank frequently and had been caught being drunk with his men, men who had been seen visiting brothels. It was claimed that women of disreputable character would at times visit the chateau grounds and that Kingston even let his men run their own estaminets.

Kingston confessed to Allen that he did drink with his men on occasion and would pay for their drinks, just as they would sometimes pay for his. The purpose of this was to get along with his men. Having a drink with them and being sociable appeared the best way to achieve a good understanding of his subordinates.

It was no secret that Kingston and his men were regular visitors at Suzanne's estaminet. There was no other source of entertainment at Villers-Bretonneux, Kingston explained, so what else could he expect his men to do? Most of them were young blokes involved in an extremely ugly job on a daily basis. Having fun with the friendly French girls while enjoying a drink made them forget the work for a few hours. Kingston could not see the harm in it, especially for the younger men like himself who had come into the army with no prior sexual experience. Some of Kingston's men did not know any other women other than the prostitutes and the French themselves did not appear to mind that the women did what they did.

Licensed brothels had existed in France since the mid-nineteenth century and during the war the trade had understandably flourished.[9] There was a hierarchy for officers and common soldiers who visited the brothels during and also after the war, with blue lamps displayed if they were for officers and red lamps for other ranks. For many of the men, visits to a brothel were considered a physical necessity and abstinence was believed to be harmful to your health. Physical need made it more acceptable for married rather than single men to visit prostitutes, but none of the young boys wanted to die a virgin. Looking to get as much out of life as they could, men would regularly spend what might well be their final mortal hours in a brothel. It could also be a way to avoid death for a time—if they came down with a venereal disease, they would be able to swap the trenches for a few weeks in hospital.

Kingston did not think that what was going on in Villers-Bretonneux or any other part of France where soldiers were still stationed was in any way problematic. It was only a continuation of what had been looked upon as a fairly normal activity during the war. Yes, his men were friendly with the many women who had once entertained the thousands of soldiers returning from the battlefields. Charlie Kingston let Alfred Allen know that he did not think of it as a crime and he did not understand why Lee was making such an issue of it. It wasn't as if Lee's own men were living in celibacy.

Poperinghe, where Allen was based, had Talbot House, an institution that had come about when British Army chaplains Neville Talbot and Philip 'Tubby' Clayton decided to open a men's club in the town.[10] It was meant to provide the soldiers, regardless of their rank, with some entertainment, a place they could come to after the mud and the madness of the battlefield. It also provided an alternative for the rather controversial nightlife the town otherwise offered. During the evenings small cabaret groups, like the Happy Hoppers, would entertain, but it was mainly a British affair where women, beer and brandy were excluded. What it did offer those visiting was a library, tea, a large tranquil walled garden where men could sit and listen to the birds in the trees, and a chapel in the attic. Although for many it was a relaxing retreat, for the post-war soldiers under Charlie Kingston's command the place was not popular.

In Villers-Bretonneux there was very little in the way of entertainment in the ruined town, and no Talbot House or its equivalent. Captain Spedding had done his utmost for the men in trying to obtain cinema equipment from the local YMCA but this request had been refused. Instead, a billiard table was sent to the chateau and a couple of weeks later a piano and a few tennis racquets arrived.[11] That was it. There was nothing in the way of amusement except for the bars and the friendly women. Kingston believed that even if they had had a Talbot (or 'Toc. H', as it was referred to), his men would probably not have chosen to go there. Some who had visited Poperinghe came back with stories about boring evenings there, with no women and no alcohol. A nice place for the goody-two-shoes and the English, but for everyone else as boring as a bus ride on a wet day.

Allen warned Kingston that he was breaching military rules by letting women spend time with his men in their huts. That immorality was looked upon as a military offence surprised Kingston, and he let Allen know that he had never heard of such a thing. Besides, the chateau grounds were open, and it was impossible to prevent men from bringing women onto the camp grounds.[12] Shrugging at Allen, he said, 'What am I supposed to do?'

Allen did not dislike Kingston. The man had been accommodating towards him. He was a young man in charge of a group of ex-soldiers for the first time in his life, a responsibility he had never held before. Allen could clearly understand how the antagonism between Kingston and Lee had developed, but he could not understand why they both acted like petulant children. Especially Lee, who appeared to want to go to extremes to get his way with his constant whining. It was becoming annoying and causing problems.

Allen thought it would be best to ignore Lee and hope the whole thing would blow over, but he would talk to General Hobbs about it. It might be wise to send Lee back to England for demobilisation. That might solve a lot of problems.

Then he got a phone call. It was from the AIF. It appeared that another party had now come forward making serious allegations of fraudulent behaviour by Kingston. Driver Willoughby Bollen had been staying in the chateau grounds with his family for the past few months and he had sent a letter to London, complaining about the behaviour of the Australian men and of Kingston in particular. He was demanding an official inquiry and the AIF was taking his allegations very seriously. In fact, they were considering granting Bollen an inquiry.

When Allen took it up with him, Kingston realised matters were about to become extremely messy and, at best, highly embarrassing.

Chapter 5
WILLOUGHBY RICHARD BOLLEN

Willoughby Richard Bollen was furious.

At the end of the war Bollen had not wanted to return to Australia, realising that his working options in the military would be much more rewarding than any job he might secure as a civilian. So he had applied through Australia House to become a driver in the newly established Australian Graves Services and was taken on.[1] Before he left London he signed a document stating that he would be engaged by the AGS for at least two years or until such time that his services were terminated. On 25 November 1919, he reported to Captain Kingston in France. His duty was to be the driver of one of the two ambulances at Villers-Bretonneux.

Assuming he would be in France for at least a couple of years, he made arrangements for his wife, her sister and his fourteen-year-old son to travel from Melbourne to France. After his family arrived, he enrolled his boy into a French school in the hope that this would widen the lad's future career opportunities.

The accommodations in the grounds were very poor. The chateau's owner, Madame Delacour, had reclaimed her buildings just before the start of the winter. It meant that Bollen would have to build his own living quarters on the chateau grounds. His hut would have to be bigger and in better condition than the huts that had been built already to house four people, two of them women. One of the new drivers let Bollen know that there was an abandoned British POW camp just a few miles up the road that appeared to be in quite good nick.

So in the weeks that followed, Will Bollen, together with two other new drivers, went to work dismantling two of the huts and a larger shed in the deserted camp and used this material to construct makeshift huts for the two drivers and a larger home for the Bollen family. Although these quarters were better than the rickety ones the other men lived in, the hut remained a cold, windy and damp affair during the winter months. The Bollens did their utmost to make their hut cosy, furnishing it with beds, chairs, tables and even a few paintings they had brought with them from Australia. All the cracks were filled with old newspapers and, with a forest in the grounds, there was enough wood to feed their log burner. They also had unlimited access to oil and petrol.

Nonetheless, the hut remained a very small space for four people of different ages to live in, and at times Bollen's wife, Janet, would get crabby and could be heard shouting at her husband. The other men teased Bollen about his bossy wife and Bollen tried to take the jokes in his stride, but it did make him feel self-conscious.

By February 1920, Bollen's son was doing very well at school. However, dark clouds were now gathering over his reasonably happy family. It had become apparent to Bollen that if Captain Kingston got his way, he and his family would very soon be demobilised and sent back to Australia.

Bollen didn't actually know what had started it all. Somewhere along the way his relationship with the men, especially Kingston, had gone sour. After his wife and child arrived he complained about the numerous ladies visiting the camp and the constant drunkenness of the men. For Bollen the camp had taken on the appearance of an open brothel and he feared it would have a bad influence on his teenage son.

He'd had some run-ins with the men, but it had all grown curiously out of hand when he collided with another car, badly damaging the ambulance he was driving. Kingston made an enormous fuss about this, claiming that Bollen wasn't taking care of his vehicle appropriately and that he was an incompetent driver. Kingston took Bollen off the ambulance as a result.[2] The other drivers could often be seen tinkering with their cars, looking under their bonnets, checking motors and tyres. Bollen did no such things with his vehicle. If it broke down, he would take it to the unit's mechanic. He reasoned that he had been employed to drive the thing, not to foster it.

A week later, Bollen had developed a small pimple on his face that looked inflamed. Afraid it might turn into a boil, he had visited Kingston and asked for a leave pass to visit a doctor.

Kingston closely scrutinised the inflamed pimple and told his driver to visit Frank Carr first.[3] Sergeant Carr was the only man on the premises with any medical knowledge. He was in no way a doctor, but he'd had some medical training in the past and anyone on the grounds who was ailing had to go through Carr first. If Carr advised a visit to a real doctor then Kingston would write out a pass for the patient. The nearest medical post with a doctor on site was at Poulainville, some five miles from Amiens.

Some men in the unit had already ridiculed Bollen on occasion; when they got wind of the pimple business it became the focus of more mockery. The men began to provoke Bollen, saying that the unfortunate driver had most likely contracted gonorrhoea. Bollen was appalled by this accusation and things got worse when some men claimed that even his son had become infected. They were purposely suggesting that the son's adolescent pimples were the same as his father's now steadily growing boil.

Bollen went to Kingston to complain about these insinuations, asking his CO to put a stop to the rumours. Kingston told him he'd look into it, but of course he didn't, mainly because Kingston thought Bollen was a notorious grumbler. The Bollens—Will, as well as his wife—were always nitpicking and carrying on about the behaviour of the men, how things were being run, the cold, the drinking—about everything in general.[4] Some of the men had even told Bollen to his face that while he was living on the chateau grounds, he would either have to put up with them or piss off. Kingston fully agreed with them.

The pimple on Will Bollen's face was now gradually becoming bigger and bigger. It had done what Bollen had feared it would—turned into a contused boil. He returned to Frank Carr, who took another look at it and said he would need to lance it. It was all terribly painful and Carr told Bollen that the wound would need to be tended to, drained with boiled water and bandaged regularly. Bollen didn't sleep for four nights and could hardly lie down because of the pain. For the highly unpopular Bollen, matters got worse when he was offered and accepted help from a debatable party. The Germans.

—■—

France was one of the last nations to return its captured Germans; for this reason, there were still some prisoners of war remaining in Villers-Bretonneux for a long time after the war ended. They had helped to construct the huts and did odd jobs for the Australians, including cooking. Will Bollen and Janet, his wife, became friends with some of them. One, Friedrich Hemlin, was living on the grounds of the chateau and he would often help out in the mess. He was treated fairly well, although he was sometimes made fun of.

A couple of Australians had taken him out one night and, to make sure he did not look out of place, had dressed him in an Australian uniform before heading into one of the town's estaminets for a drink.[5] Everyone had laughed and made fun of his peculiar German accent and he just laughed along with the men, not wanting to provoke anyone. Knowing he would be sent home as soon as his papers came through, he decided to sit out his time with the Australians and try to stay on the good side of his former enemies.

Friedrich had built up a relationship of sorts with the Bollen family. He had helped Bollen put up his hut and been given a meal as a reward. He was a young chap and he took a liking to Bollen's sister-in-law, Jane. This had not gone unnoticed by the other men; Jane and Friedrich could often be seen having a friendly chat on the grounds. Jane had also taken a shine to the well-mannered German.

Friedrich was a complete gentleman compared to the Australians, Jane told her sister. When Friedrich heard about Bollen's face and the pain he was in, he told Jane that he might be able to help. Still in possession of his medical kit, which had been issued to all German soldiers, he asked if he might put some ointment on the wound. To do so he was invited into the house along with another German friend. The two men were known on the grounds as Yapp and Sapp; the Australians had given them these nicknames, claiming that their German names were too hard to pronounce.[6] For Bollen and his wife it confirmed their belief that the men on the unit were in the business of belittling those most vulnerable.

Friedrich would come in and disinfect and dress the wound. Sitting by the fire afterwards, they would all enjoy a drink and a chat. Needless to say, this chummy friendship with the 'Boche' did not go down well with the other men. Although the war was over, the Germans remained the enemy. The men claimed that Bollen's wife and her sister could be seen regularly walking down the streets of Villers-Bretonneux in the company of the German prisoners.

When Kingston spoke to Bollen about this, Bollen said that

the men were only helping to carry his wife's groceries.[7] Kingston replied that he wasn't very pleased about Bollen being hospitable toward the Germans, but Bollen told his CO that hospitality had nothing to do with it—he was grateful to the Germans for tending to his face when nobody else appeared to care. Anyway, who was Kingston to accuse him of anything?

When the discussion turned into a heated row, Bollen accused Kingston of getting drunk four times a week. It was this that provoked Kingston into wanting to get rid of this meddlesome troublemaker. When Bollen heard that Kingston was going to send him back to London, for no other reason than that he had complained about his superior's conduct, he was furious.

From the very beginning Bollen had regarded Kingston's behaviour as being far below what could and must be expected from an officer. The captain drank and let prostitutes onto the chateau grounds to entertain his men. Bollen himself was no saint and did not deny frequently drinking more than one pint of an evening, but Kingston was supposed to set an example. Bollen had done little to conceal his irritation at the way Kingston led his unit; he had complained to Kingston about this many times.

When Bollen had been living alone on the grounds he'd been able to accept how things were organised, but when his family joined him, his irritation had grown. Living on the grounds with his wife, her sister and a child, surrounded by a rough group of soldiers, proved challenging. Bollen wasn't the only one living in the compound with his wife, but he was the only one with a child and a young female relative as well.

With his three family members to consider, Will Bollen thought he should explicitly address the situation. He could not allow his family to live in such a corrupt environment, he told Kingston. The captain laughed at him and called him an 'old grumbler' to his face.

Fearing loss of their carefree way of life, the other men started complaining about Bollen's constant moaning. Bollen was aware that an officer by the name of Major Allen had been stationed in Belgium; because this man outranked Kingston, Bollen thought of seeking his help before he went directly to the AIF. Bollen had already talked to Lee about Kingston's behaviour; Lee told him he wasn't surprised, but that he could expect nothing from the 'major' in Poperinghe as Allen had no say over the units in France. Allen wasn't an AIF man, Lee explained; he himself had sought Allen's help but, when he complained about Kingston, Allen had taken no notice of him. So Bollen turned to the only person he thought would listen to him: the officer in command of the Australian Graves Services in France.

During the war, most of the officers placed with the AGD were there because they were unfit for active duty. As far as Bollen was concerned, Kingston was unfit for any duty whatsoever and he told Spedding as much. His efforts to be a respectable husband and father had resulted in him and his family becoming a target of the scorn and ridicule of the men in his unit. Captain Spedding appeared irritated at having to deal with this problem and simply told Bollen 'to just get on with it', leaving it at that.

Spedding by this time knew that he would be returning to Australia shortly and did not actually take much notice of

Bollen's complaints. A new OC by the name of George Phillips was already making his way from Lewes to London. He could deal with the matter.

—■—

In the days that followed, Bollen continued to suffer from the lanced boil. In pain and not being able to sleep for days, he returned to Kingston and asked for a pass to go to the doctor in Poulainville for treatment. Kingston finally succumbed and gave Sergeant Carr orders to take him there. Squeezed into a waiting vehicle along with four friends of Carr's, Bollan was driven to Poulainville on a Saturday evening.

The Indian doctor, Amir Singh, had been at Poulainville for some years. He had been a witness when the body of the infamous airman the 'Red Baron' had been transported to a hangar at Poulainville. Manfred von Richthofen, the son of a Prussian nobleman, had terrorised the skies over the Western Front in an Albatross biplane, downing fifteen enemy planes by the end of 1916. Von Richthofen surpassed all flying ace records on both sides of the Western Front and began using a Fokker triplane, painted entirely red in tribute to his old cavalry regiment, flying the plane during the last eight months of his life before he was shot down and killed near Amiens in April 1918.

When Bollen and Carr arrived at the hospital grounds, they made their way to Dr Singh's office. While Bollen was sent into the examining room, Carr explained to Singh the situation regarding Bollen and the boil on his face. Singh asked Carr if he would wait while he examined Bollen, but Carr appeared confused and somewhat reluctant to do so. Australians sometimes had difficulty with his Indian accent, so Singh once more explained that he wanted Carr to wait until he had examined the man he had brought in.[8]

Carr went on to explain to Singh that Bollen's son appeared to suffer from the same disease, and that it was probably contagious and liable to spread through the whole camp. He asked the doctor if Bollen could remain at the hospital, but Singh told Carr that he wanted to examine his patient before detaining him and explicitly expressed that he wanted Carr to wait until he had done so. If Bollen was really ill or was suffering from something contagious, Singh said he would send him to the rest house at Amiens until another specialist medical officer there had time to take a proper look at him and admit him into a hospital.

Singh then went into the examining room to look at his patient. He asked Bollen about his son, but Bollen denied that the boy was sick and told Singh that in his case it was a bout of adolescent pimples. Bollen told Singh that he suspected Carr had fabricated the lie in the hope of getting rid of him, so that Carr and his friends would be able to go off into the town.[9]

While he was in the medical hut, Bollen suddenly heard the car starting up. The doctor ran outside in an effort to stop the men, calling after the car as it left skid marks on the road. Singh switched on his examining torch and waved it, but the car didn't stop and soon disappeared into the distance. 'Why would they play such a dirty trick on you?' the doctor asked, returning to the medical hut.[10] Bollen shrugged and looked unhappy. He suspected that Frank Carr and his mates would head straight for Amiens, in a search of women and alcohol.

Singh did not drink or indulge in women. He didn't understand the behaviour of most Europeans, but he was able to get along with them. He had heard talk of dubious behaviour on the part of the Australians, but he had not experienced any such thing himself.

Singh was just one of the 130,000 Muslims, Hindus and Sikhs who had fought on the Western Front. By the end of the hostilities 9000 of them had lost their lives. Singh had been a witness to the first battle of Ypres, when Khudadad Khan used his machine-gun position to hold the Allied line and prevent a final German breakthrough. When the position was finally overrun, the defenders were all killed, except for Khan, who suffered many wounds and was left for dead. Despite his injuries he managed to crawl back to his own lines when darkness fell. Together with his men he then was able to hold the line long enough for further reinforcements to arrive, winning the battle as a result. For his courage and bravery Khan was awarded the Victoria Cross.

The man with the sore on his face was telling Singh that he wished to return to Villers-Bretonneux. His wife would be worried and she would probably wait up for him, he said—probably all night if he didn't come back. The doctor, understanding the man's predicament, offered him a ride with his own driver, who could take him as far as Amiens. Bollen would have to walk the other ten miles, and although the wound on Bollen's face caused the doctor some concern, he thought the man fit enough to walk the distance. Singh had checked him thoroughly and had not found any other ailments.

Grateful for the offer, Bollen climbed into the car next to the driver. But as soon as the driver started the engine it became evident that something was wrong. When the driver climbed out to see what the trouble was he noticed that the exhaust pipe was gone.[11] Wondering where it had gone, he searched under the car and around the area, but the pipe had vanished. Bollen had his own idea about who the culprit might have been.

The driver decided he would still drive Bollen to Amiens. The lack of an exhaust pipe didn't interfere with driving the car, although you could hear it was gone. All the way to Amiens it made a terrible racket and they could hardly talk as they drove along. It was dark by the time they got to Amiens, where Bollen got out.

As Bollen disembarked, he saw a familiar car standing outside the red-light area. Carr and his mates were probably wearing out the girls there. Well, he wasn't planning on confronting them and then asking for a ride home. With no intention of stooping so low, he made up his mind to walk the ten miles back to Villers-Bretonneux.

His wife was waiting for him when he got home. Upset and very annoyed that no one had taken the trouble to go by her hut and explain to her that Bollen had been left behind at Poulainville, she told her husband that she would take the matter up with Kingston in the morning.

The next day, before Janet could confront Captain Kingston with what had happened the night before, he called Bollen in and let him know that his work had been deemed unsatisfactory. Kingston was applying for his discharge from the army. Bollen was furious and demanded an explanation. Kingston told him that he was lazy, had been sick for over a fortnight, that the other men did not like him and that out of the five months he had been there he had only put in two and a half months of work. Kingston also did not like the way Bollen and his family were fraternising with the German prisoners. Kingston explained that he had been given orders, issued by Australia House, to discharge some of his men due to the need to cut back the numbers of AGS personnel.

Bollen felt victimised. He was shocked and felt that everyone in the camp had turned against him. Leaving him at Poulainville was a mean, despicable trick played on him by others, and now he felt he was paying the price because he had obviously rubbed some people up the wrong way. He decided that he had suffered enough. Hoping for justice in what he viewed as a grossly unfair situation, Bollen resolved to write a letter to the AIF. In it he would explain exactly what was going on in France.

Chapter 6
GEORGE LORT PHILLIPS

As part of the 13th Battalion, George Lort Phillips landed at Gallipoli on 25 April 1915.[1] For the Australians it was their first real taste of warfare. Overnight on 2 May, they lost eight officers and 330 men. At roll call on 3 May, only a couple of officers and 290 men answered their names.

The August Offensive was a major attempt by Allied forces at Gallipoli to break the stalemate that had persisted since the landings on 25 April 1915. In an attempt to seize high points along the Sari Bair range, the offensive began on 6 August with a diversionary attack by Anzacs at Lone Pine, a British attack on The Vineyard at Helles and British landings at Suvla Bay. Phillips had been there when the offensive led to disaster as Turkish troops, under the command of Colonel Mustafa Kemal, counterattacked, driving the Allied troops from Chunuk Bair and holding steady against all the diversionary attacks.

It was there that shrapnel hit Phillips in the shoulder and leg. Immobile due to his wounds, he had watched the soldiers around him perish by the dozens. When the medics were finally able to get to him, they said he was lucky to have survived because he was bleeding profusely from his ankle and shoulder. Loading him onto a stretcher, the medics took him to a field hospital but, due to the severity of his wounds, he was later transported to a hospital in Alexandria.

His shoulder had to be drained and the joint in his left ankle was shattered; to add to his misery, both injuries became infected during his stay in hospital. His ankle had to be reopened and his shoulder drained again. After six months of hospitalisation, Phillips was finally discharged. He left the hospital a disabled man at the age of 24. He would need a walking stick for the rest of his life and had also lost the use of his left arm. The doctors told him he would probably continue to suffer from chronic pain in both limbs throughout his life. After his discharge, it became obvious that Phillips would never see active duty again, so he was shipped off to London and put to work as an administrator at the AIF headquarters at Horseferry Road in London.

In 1917 Phillips was promoted to the rank of major and made governor of the AIF Detention Barracks at Lewes, near Brighton in Sussex.[2] Lewes Civil Gaol had been taken over by the AIF on 1 November 1917 and it was still being used in 1919 as a detention barracks for Australian soldiers. Phillips was known as an excellent disciplinarian and was also praised by his superiors for his knowledge of, and sympathy with, human nature. In 1918 he met 29-year-old Lilian Ansel. Their marriage was formalised at St James Westminster Church in London on 30 October 1919.

At the end of January 1920 Phillips was asked to take over the task of officer in charge of the Australian Graves Services, preferably as soon as possible. Captain Spedding had somewhat unexpectedly resigned his appointment and would be leaving for Australia. Rumours had been spreading that the Australian Graves Services in France were not functioning adequately and that there had been a number of complaints made by men serving there. Faced with serious allegations and a request for an inquiry to be held, High Commissioner Andrew Fisher was forced to ask Phillips to hold up the light to the officers on duty in France and also the staff at Australia House.

Fisher wanted to make sure that the men under his command in London would not be tainted by any wrongdoing if such an actual inquiry were to come about. He was opposed to any official inquiry being held, but he was not sure if he would be able to prevent it if Senator Pearce, who was now Australia's minister for defence, got involved. If the situation was really as bad as the letters sent to the AIF had implied then some kind of inquiry would need to be established, if only to exonerate the good name of the military.

Fisher understandably wanted to keep things as low-key as he could, and he let Phillips know how he felt. Just a year ago there had been a public outcry when newspaper articles had detailed how the graves of Australians buried at Gallipoli had been desecrated. At that time historian Charles Bean had been sent over to check up on things.[3]

Charles Bean, Australia's official war historian, had been a journalist for *The Sydney Morning Herald* before the war.[4] Bean was born in Australia, but his family moved back to England in 1890. In 1891 his father became headmaster of Brentwood School in Essex. Ever since the early 1890s, when his father had taken a ten-year-old Charles to the battlefield of Waterloo, he had been fascinated by the relics of warfare. Bean became a special correspondent for the *Herald* and in mid-1914 was given the job of writing a daily article about the gathering crisis in Europe. In September, the Imperial government invited each dominion to attach an official correspondent to its forces. The Australian minister for defence, George Pearce, invited the Australian Journalists' Association to nominate a man, and in a ballot of members Bean won narrowly from Keith Murdoch of the Melbourne *Herald*.

Travelling to Egypt with the first contingent of Australian troops, Bean was there when they landed at Gallipoli on 25 April. Shot in the leg during the hostilities, he refused to return home and stayed in his dugout until the wound had healed, all the time writing about the battle. Bean was very accurate in his reports and even revealed that some men were discharged and sent home for bad conduct. This annoyed quite a few of the soldiers, although Bean also wrote about the sacrifice of the troops, their bravery and the number of men who had fallen. Bean was such a demon for accuracy that some people believed that he actually counted the bullets that passed him each day in the field. During the war he became Australia's conscience.

After his visit to the gravesites at Gallipoli, Bean claimed that although locals had stolen some of the wooden crosses, removing them from the graves to use as firewood, the condition of the gravesite had not overly shocked him. Yes, the cemetery was not in as good nick as it should have been, with crosses missing and others in disarray due to weather conditions, but the site had been restored while Bean was there and he sent back reassuring photos of a graveyard that looked well cared for.

Fisher did not want another outcry. The AIF had just finished dealing with a case of fraud, involving blank leave passes and allowances.[5] There had been a whole mess concerning six AIF men who had managed to steal at least two blank pass-books, each containing a hundred leave passes and a hundred passes for ration allowances from a depository located at St George's Square in Pimlico. Fictitious names were signed to the passes and in 84 cases money had been paid out to the person who had presented the pass. It had been hard to prove in court because the conspirators had stuck together. In the end, the suspects had been sent back to Australia with a slap on the wrist.

Although Fisher was not directly responsible for the men serving with the AIF, he knew he would be held accountable for the actions of the men in the AGS. If it was all as bad as it appeared, he truly feared for the continuation of his appointment in London. Already the quality of his administration at Australia House had come under scrutiny. Some of it was due to his ill health—he often suffered from 'nervous tiredness', while hereditary heart problems left him unable to work at times. With his six young children running around the house Fisher seldom found any tranquillity. The coldness and dampness of English weather wasn't doing him any good either, but some of the problems he was facing in the office were also due to post-war administrative adjustments.[6]

It was true that his influence in London wasn't very highly regarded by Australian Prime Minister Billy Hughes. Fisher did not fit in well with the British political establishment; he was no good at flattery and was known as a left radical. The much-appreciated English taste for decorum was wasted on Fisher. On top of that, the government in Australia was probing him and complaining about the mounting war debt. By 1920 it had mounted to 335 million pounds and his London funds were being curtailed. Fisher feared the Australian Economics Commission, initiated to control departmental waste, might even go so far as to institute an investigation into his department.

There was also another matter that caused him concern. Just weeks before, at the beginning of January 1920, news leaked out that the OC at Australia House, Quentin Spedding, had approved a request from a French family concerning the remains of one of their family members. The corpse of the Frenchman became known as 'The Duke' to the men.[7]

The Duke, an aristocrat, had been killed near the Somme and his family was aware of the location of his remains. They dearly wanted their son reinterred in the family vault. The 'Ware Rule' decreed that all soldiers, regardless of rank, must be buried side by side in designated cemeteries. There could and would be no exception made for those who had enough power and money to make possible what others who did not have access to these privileges could not. However, The Duke's family were French and wanted their son to come home. They had the money to make it happen, and the power. In pursuit of their fervent wishes, they approached the Australians who worked together with the British exhumation teams.

Spedding received a pleading letter from them along with a sum of money. He approached William Lee to help in locating the grave and organising an exhumation, so that the family would be able to take their son's remains home. However, French officers got wind of it before the body could be unearthed and immediately reported the matter to the Australian authorities.

Fisher suspected that it had been nothing more than an act of bad judgement on Spedding's part. Spedding was known as a bristly OC who did not always play by the book, but Fisher believed there had been no dishonesty involved. The OC had merely been trying to help the family. When Fisher probed him about it, Spedding assured him he had not acted out of gain. He had assumed that there would not be any problem in reinterring The Duke because he was French and not a Commonwealth subject. Still, Fisher did not like the idea of one of his staff accepting money from the family. This was very much against the rules of the AGS.

Despite Spedding's explanation, Fisher deemed the matter serious enough to ask him to make the honourable decision and to step down from the AGS. If this matter resurfaced during an official inquiry, Fisher feared his own position as high commissioner, a position he dearly loved, might come under serious threat. Fisher had a large family to support and no other means of income.

The AGS men in France, getting wind that Spedding would soon be replaced, quickly drew up a petition to keep Spedding in office. Many of them signed it, but to no avail. Spedding could leave quietly, Fisher said, maintaining his rank, keeping his job as an AIF officer without having to face any repercussions. Fisher let him know that he might even be employed in some other capacity in the future. Spedding had no choice but to step down, honourably. Whenever asked about it later, he referred to the matter as a small 'error of judgment' on his part.[8]

—■—

Taking over the job at the AGS office, Phillips discovered he had been left with a gravely dysfunctional unit.[9] Correspondence was not up to date and a number of civilian staff members had not had their duties properly delegated to them. During the first week he got the impression that the department had not been run professionally for some time.

In France, no inventories were made. There were no lists of what had come in and what had gone out of the stores. The general system had been worked by a number of non-commissioned officers and, as a result, no proper accounting had been made, except for a very rough list of clothes and other small items. Keys to the stores seemed to belong to whoever wanted them.

When Phillips started his reorganisation, he was quick to take in those keys, leaving just three to be used by the office staff members in charge at Poperinghe, Amiens and Villers-Bretonneux. Phillips also made it clear that, together with the quartermaster, these officers in charge would now become responsible for keeping the books.

All this did not make Phillips popular, but that did not deter him. During his time in charge of a prison he had become used to taking unpopular measures. Phillips represented the military police, who, to the fighting men, had been as much the enemy as any German was. Regarded as men who had turned on their own, the MPs were shunned by their fellow soldiers and countrymen. The 'jacks', as they were nicknamed by the soldiers, were not well liked and anyone connected to them was met with a fair dose of suspicion and contempt. Phillips knew he would be walking a tightrope as OC of the AGS, but he had walked tightropes before and he was not afraid of falling.

After starting work at Australia House, Phillips quickly discovered that the seventeen female clerks working as secretaries and typists at Australia House appeared to have no work ethic at all: they walked in and out of the office as they pleased, and indulged in lengthy gossip sessions. No one appeared to be in any way impressed or daunted by his presence when Phillips entered their office. They carried on with their gossip and only reluctantly went on with their work when he rebuked them. He found that his staff considered him a pest that had unexpectedly landed on them; he believed that some of them hoped he would in time vanish as suddenly as he had arrived.

It took Phillips all of three weeks to get the situation under control. He discovered that the AGS was badly overstaffed, so he discharged a couple of AIF people at Australia House. It was intended that the AGS would over time become a civilian department so to discharge the AIF people first was an understandable decision, but it did not earn him any credit and only inflamed the rumour that the military police were taking over the AGS. Phillips had heard such rumours meandering through the corridors at Australia House. Those who were muttering them would quickly move away when he approached.

Quentin Spedding was furious when he heard that Major Phillips had accused him of leaving the graves section behind him in disarray. It was hard to take this seriously. The assistant secretary of the High Commissioner's Office, Colonel George Justice Hogben, himself had informed Spedding that his work had been very satisfactory.[10] Now he found himself being stabbed in the back by someone who had taken his place, an untrustworthy MP fellow who had marched into the AGS offices and who was now besmirching his good name.

Spedding claimed to those around him that, through the intercession of High Commissioner Fisher, he had been offered a job with the defence department in Australia after his resignation from the AGS. According to Spedding, he was not in a situation to reveal much about his new job because it concerned a 'special mission'.[11] If the job was ever promised to him it never turned into anything; when he returned to Australia, he was transferred to the Australian Army Reserve and soon returned to his old profession as a journalist working for *The Daily Telegraph*.

Spedding was proud of the work he had achieved at Australia House. When he was first employed the AGS had been nothing more than an outline of an idea, and, over the period of a few months he had managed to create a functioning organisation. It may have had its flaws, but these would have been straightened out if only he had had the chance to carry on with his work. Overall, he thought he had not done a bad job of it.

The AGS had not come into being all at once. It had required a lot of pioneering work and considerable energy and labour to bring it up to its present status. This could not be achieved in a month, or even several months. It was still an ongoing project, and he did not like all the insinuations and allegations that were arising about the way he had conducted himself. All he had ever wanted and attempted was to see the work carried out successfully.

Shortly after taking over from Spedding, Major Phillips received a report from one of his officers, a Major Allen, about complaints from Billy Lee concerning Charlie Kingston. Allen said he had investigated the matter but he had found no irregularities to support the allegations and went on to let Phillips know that he considered Lee's services had from time to time been more than unsatisfactory. Allen described Lee as a 'disturbing element' to his new OC.[12] It would be wise to replace the man.

Allen also explained to Phillips that, as far as he was concerned, the troubles in France originated from lack of supervision. How could one expect a service to function if there were no proper instructions or control? The situation in France had escalated thanks to poor supervision from Australia House and because there was no one who held supreme control over discipline and organisation in France.

Phillips quickly formed a favourable impression of Allen, who to him seemed a level-headed and amiable man, a man who did not judge Phillips because of his past as governor of a detention barrack. Of course, the major was a civilian and wasn't tainted by prejudice where military matters were concerned. Phillips did not have many friends, so Allen became something of a confidante. Phillips did not object that Allen used his honorary rank of major to introduce himself. What he had observed in regard to the man's work had been very satisfactory thus far and Poperinghe, his base, appeared to be running very smoothly. Allen was quick to assist Phillips in dealing with problems, giving him advice and offering solutions.

On one of Phillips' first visits to Poperinghe as OC of the AGS, Allen informed him that one of Kingston's men, a photographer called William Fredrick Edwards, and one of Lee's men, drafts-man Sergeant George Coughlan, were running estaminets.[13] The officers decided it would be best to address this together right away. The signal would let the men know that a new broom was sweeping through the AGS and that those running the show were not going to put up with any more disobedience. They set out for France to confront the men.

Bill Edwards had come to the AGS in September 1919. He thought he was going to be a clerk, but he soon found himself toting a camera. Having no experience whatsoever of photography as a science, with the exception of having taken a photo or two with a Kodak Junior 1A, Edwards initially turned for advice to one of his friends who had joined the photographic section and was already experienced in the field.

Edwards did his work without any real sense of dedication. To most serving in the photography unit, taking pictures wasn't very rewarding work. They never saw the results of their day in the field. Once they took the photograph and filled their rolls, the film would be sent off to London to be developed. If the photos were good they hardly ever got any feedback; but if they were no good, they would be notified and have to go back and do it all over again.

Most of the photographers, including Edwards, only photographed about four graves a day on average. Once the unit had been set up it was almost winter, and with the cold and rain the motivation to go out into those dreary fields wasn't high on anyone's list. The cameras they worked with weren't bad but, if the lighting was poor, then without training it was almost impossible to take a proper photo. Because of the lack of work, Edwards got bored, and, being an enterprising young man, he was quick to spot a job that was not only entertaining but also earned him some money.

When Allen and Phillips showed up unexpectedly, Edwards was caught red-handed working behind the bar at an estaminet. Not only that but he was also fully dressed in an Australian uniform. In an effort to explain his presence behind the bar, Edwards told Phillips and Allen that he intended to marry the owner of the estaminet. Feigning indignation, he explained that he wished to settle permanently in France with his lady friend who owned the place. He was just helping her out, he said; there was nothing to it really, it wasn't as if he was earning anything. He was wearing his uniform because he had just come home from a photographic mission.

Allen and Phillips weren't buying it. Even if Edwards' story was true, he was still overstepping the rules. They told Edwards that he was now officially under open arrest. He was to report to Kingston the next day and they told him he could start preparing for demobilisation, providing he was not court-martialled first.

That same evening Allen and Phillips proceeded to the estaminet where Sergeant George Coughlan was rumoured to be working. Coughlan had been selected personally by Spedding to serve as a draftsman in the AGS. With all the new cemeteries being created there was a need for competent draftsmen in the AGS. Working for his father, Coughlan had learned drawing and surveying. Although he actually wasn't licensed, he drew plans for cemeteries around Amiens, going out with Captain Lee to do so. There were days when they would survey two cemeteries a day. The actual surveying wasn't hard to do, but Coughlan mostly needed to measure everything himself. In all he had surveyed about 29 possible cemeteries since he joined the AGS.

He had, however, copied most of the survey plans from already existing blueprints of the cemeteries in the area that he had got hold of at the Méaulte town hall, a small town near Amiens. Tracing the existing outlines of the blueprints as best he could, he'd send them off to Australia House, signing his own name to the document. He did not see any harm in it. Of course, he sometimes had to extend or decrease the size of the plan to fit the land it was to be created on. One size did not always fit all, but using his own common sense and craftsmanship he managed to get by.

A few months after the AGS had taken him on, Coughlan started living with a woman who ran a hotel at Amiens. The woman was known by the soldiers as 'Maltese Molly' and she was a popular, albeit somewhat older, prostitute[14] who was working from an old hotel on the boulevard. After she met Coughlan she sold the hotel and with the money bought a new estaminet. For a while Coughlan told Lee that he was only renting a room there and in his free time he was sometimes helping out behind the bar, but he had actually signed his name to a document that made him the legal owner of the estaminet. It wasn't a big deal, he explained to Allen and Phillips—he helped out washing glasses and handing over beer and the madame, Marguerite Maultese, let him rent a room cheaply. He was lying through his teeth, though, and Coughlan, as well as his two superiors, knew it. He was living with a woman who was a prostitute and Phillips suspected Coughlan had become Maltese Molly's pimp.

Coughlan denied this vehemently. He was deeply in love with his Marguerite, he claimed. He had even almost lost his life over her when a crazed man had come after him. Another member of the AGS, Sergeant Robert Shaw, had befriended Maltese Molly before Coughlan came on the scene and he had thought the attraction was mutual. Shaw had boasted that he and Molly were soon to be married and that she would stop selling her body for money once they did. But then Molly met Coughlan and, when Shaw found out the sergeant had pinched his sweetheart, he was beside himself with anger and grief. Shaw swore he'd kill Coughlan and he almost did.

Coming back to the estaminet late one night, Coughlan was stopped on the road by someone in a car. He only realised who it was when Shaw stepped out of the car with a gun in his hand. Shaw had pointed the gun very steadily at Coughlan and aimed at his chest, Ned Kelly style. Coughlan kept his hands raised in the air as a sign of surrender and prayed to God that Shaw would not pull the trigger. The two stood there—one of them ranting, almost foaming at the mouth, while the other tried fervently to calm him down.[15]

After a few minutes, Shaw thought the better of it and lowered his gun. But his anger still needed an outlet, so he stepped up to his rival and floored him with a punch to the face. After that Shaw stepped back into the car and drove off, leaving his trembling rival lying in the gutter with a bruised face and a somewhat dented ego. Coughlan, not wanting matters to get out of hand, did not report the incident to anyone, but two weeks later Coughlan heard that Shaw had been called back to London, to be discharged and sent home.

Coughlan, still recovering from the blow to his face, did get back at his rival. Along with his other enterprising occupations he had also started a small business selling Peter Pan cigarettes. They had most likely been stolen from the Australian storeroom in Amiens. When another officer caught him red-handed selling the cigarettes from behind the counter, he put the blame on Shaw. He said that a girl Shaw had dated had offered them to Coughlan after Shaw left for London. Nonetheless, Coughlan had been officially reprimanded for this offence.

Now, confronted by Allen and Phillips, Coughlan realised that he was not going to be able to lie himself out of this mess. The cigarette business had been dealt with just weeks ago; now, as he stood in the doorway in his pyjamas, he realised that he was quickly running out of arguments and soon stopped trying to defend himself. Allen and Phillips placed George Coughlan under open arrest.

The next day Phillips and Allen paid a visit to Lee's office in Amiens. They told him that one of his men was running an estaminet and living with a prostitute, but Lee appeared unfazed. Lee admitted that he also lived with a woman who wasn't his wife, although this was not common knowledge to his men. He let Allen and Phillips know that one of his men named Stuart lived with a woman who ran a Chinese brothel in Corbie a small town a couple of miles up the road from Amiens.[16] What were they supposed to do? The French women didn't seem to mind being promiscuous and the Australian men certainly didn't mind them being so. In France prostitution was seen as a legal occupation.

Phillips said he was very dissatisfied with Lee's supervision and he made it clear that he was planning a total reorganisation. In view of this, Lee's services were terminated and he was to report to London the next day, along with Edwards and Coughlan. In short, he was fired.

Billy Lee travelled to London the next day, but he took his anger and indignation with him. Not he but Charlie Kingston was the one who should have been sent home, he believed, because one of his men had also been caught behind the bar wearing his uniform and Kingston's reputation was by far worse than his. Lee felt victimised and regarded his treatment as a grave injustice. Because Phillips and Allen had showed up at his office unexpectedly, he suspected that together they were in the process of systematically cleansing the AGS of any disturbing elements.

Quentin Spedding, Billy Lee and some AIF men already suspected Alfred Allen was in the process of planning a takeover in France. Everyone knew that the AGS jobs were potentially lucrative because of the many fringe benefits—significant sums were paid out for petrol, tyres and the cost of living. Men in the AGS wanted to hang on to their jobs.

However, Phillips saw the need for someone with authority to be in charge on the continent. Phillips could not always be in France and Belgium to tend to matters; he had duties in London to attend to. There was no one else in the area who had the capacity to do the job, so in February 1920 Phillips gave Major Allen full control of the northern France area as officer in command. He appointed Charlie Kingston as Allen's assistant.

Chapter 7
ALFRED ALLEN

Who was this man, Alfred Allen? He had seemingly just tumbled into the AGS job at Poperinghe out of nowhere and most men had no idea where he had come from, except that he had not originated from the AIF but had sprouted from some religious organisation and his rank was honorary. Quentin Spedding described him as a capable man, not young and certainly not frivolous. A man who rarely spoke to a woman, except one lady who was a Red Cross driver.[1]

Alfred Allen in fact had come from a wealthy and esteemed family. He was the second son of Alfred Allen and Amelia Petford, who lived at Waverley in Sydney. Allen's family were prominent Quakers and he had two brothers and a sister. Their religion obligated them not to drink, smoke or swear.

Alfred senior became a free trader and went into politics, representing Paddington in the Legislative Assembly from 1887 to

1894. In the general election of July 1894 he stood for Waverley, but lost.

At a young age Alfred Allen junior already ran his own architect business. He had grown up realising how politics worked and how to use one's influence to step up the ladder, but he had also seen how fickle and unreliable one's status was. Nonetheless, he soon became a well-known architect around the Sydney area; among his projects were plans for a large villa residence at Woollahra, a cottage at Camden, and a bungalow and villa at Waverley.

Alfred Allen enjoyed his life in Sydney. He was a good-humoured and quite amiable person; together with his two brothers and sister, he founded the Pickwick Corresponding Club, which re-enacted scenes from Dickens' *Pickwick Papers*.[2] He appeared to read a lot, and wasn't one to go out with girls. His father, however, was a great advocate of married life and delivered long speeches on the marital obligations of wives and husbands. It therefore came as a surprise to the family when young Alfred came home with his wife to be, Ellen (Nellie) Renshaw, whom he married on 21 December 1897. Their daughter and only child, Doris Eileen, was born in February 1900.

Much to his father's dismay, young Alfred did not appear to enjoy married life one bit and did not live up to the marital obligations his father advocated. Alfred senior wasn't at all pleased to see his son put to shame what he himself held sacred. Around 1913 Allen left home to travel. The trip was meant to allow him to develop his architectural capabilities by studying buildings all around the world. Leaving Nellie behind, he took off to visit England, Ireland, Scotland, Italy and South Africa.

However, when he returned to Sydney and his married life, he did everything possible to escape his wife. Working at his architecture practice in Pitt Street, he kept long hours and would often not return home at night. As a result his wife hardly saw him.

For Alfred, another way to leave home came when World War I broke out. As a Quaker he was a conscientious objector and could not take up arms, but he joined the ambulance corps organised by the Society of Friends. Alfred had become very impressed with England during his travels and its capital, London, had stolen his heart. When the Friends offered him a position with the ambulance corps there he did not hesitate to leave for his beloved London in 1915. Shortly after his arrival, however, the Society of Friends sent him to Gouda in the Netherlands.

As a neutral party in the conflict, the Netherlands had not been affected by the war as much as the surrounding countries had. The country was considered a safe haven and so they provided refugee camps for those fleeing their countries to escape the battle. The Belgians especially were suffering the ill effects of the war along their borders. They too had resolved to stay neutral during the war, but the country had come into conflict with Germany and had become a reluctant party in the war.

Belgium lost its status of neutrality at the end of July 1914, when Germany asked the government to provide a free passage through the country into France. The Belgians refused and the German answer to this refusal was to attack the small country.

It was France that rushed in to help its tiny neighbour, 'Brave Little Belgium', and a bloody war along its borders was a result. In October 1914, when Antwerp was invaded and occupied by the Germans, a large number of Belgian refugees started pouring into the Netherlands.

Almost one million Belgians fled their homes, seeking safety in neighbouring countries. The vast numbers of refugees presented a grave problem because the Dutch at the time only had a population of six million. The government was at a loss as to how to feed and accommodate so many desperate people. A number of government refugee camps were set up around the country, in the cities Nunspeet, Uden and Ede. Gouda also set up a camp for the Belgians. Unlike the other camps, the measures in Gouda were not governmentally endorsed; they came about through private initiatives.[3]

The Belgians in Gouda sometimes found lodgings with the residents but also with a number of church-related community organisations that offered shelter to the refugees. A barge lying in the small harbour was put to use, but the largest and most unusual refugee camp was established in a number of greenhouses owned by the Steensma brothers. The Steensma family had been in the floral business but, due to the war, their business had collapsed. Because their greenhouses could be kept warm during the cold winter, the brothers decided to open them to accommodate the large numbers of homeless Belgians.

Conditions in the camp in Gouda were reasonably good under the circumstances, but the refugees faced substantial problems. They had been forced to leave their homes; most had left family members behind and they worried about their safety. In their rushed escape to the Netherlands, some people had lost contact with their loved ones, particularly elderly family members and sometimes children. There was a large influx of unaccompanied Belgian children, who were understandably distraught and traumatised.

The Society of Friends, recognising the problems the Dutch faced as the influx of refugees increased, created workshops for the refugees in Gouda and they also sent a number of their members to help out.[4] Alfred Allen was one of these and he set to work organising metal and wood workshops for the male residents. The items produced—such as baskets, and metal objects like ashtrays, toys and lamps—were shipped off to England and sold there. The thinking of the Society of Friends was that it was good to keep the Belgians busy because 'idleness would inevitably lead to mental decline'. Over the course of time some refugees began to complain about the working hours and the number of items that they were expected to produce on a daily basis; this dispute was resolved by paying workers a small amount of money.

Alfred Allen was also in charge of the recreational activities for the men's and boys' camp and he supervised other activities. The Australian Red Cross worked in conjunction with the Society of Friends and Allen became a well-known figure in those circles. He had close ties with the English Red Cross and often functioned as a liaison between the different charity organisations. The Australian Red Cross made him an honorary major in 1917, and he became assistant director for the Red Cross in the Netherlands just a year later.

An Australian journalist who interviewed Allen spoke of his cheerfulness and willingness to tackle any task. His proficiency in French, Dutch and Flemish was improving and he set to work in the fever-stricken camp where he was stationed; he was determined to set up a recreation scheme for the sick men and boys there, who were under quarantine restrictions. The journalist noted that although Allen was not involved in any fighting at the front, he was certainly 'cheering our boys on'.[5]

English-born General Talbot Hobbs had been commander of the Australian 5th Division during the war and the Australian-born Lieutenant Colonel (later Lieutenant General) Carl Jess had been commander of the 7th Battalion. Both of these distinguished leaders had met Allen when he worked as assistant director of the Red Cross. Shortly after the war, the Belgians returned to their homes and the refugee camps were abandoned, while the staff of the Society of Friends returned to London. In England in July 1919, Allen, encouraged by Hobbs, applied for a job as an architect for the gravesites in France.[6]

Soon afterwards, Allen received a telephone call from London confirming that he had been accepted by the Imperial War Graves Commission. He would go to work for the Australian Graves Services where he would be made captain and receive a salary in accordance with his rank. Working for the Red Cross, Allen had held the honorary rank of major, so in a sense it was a downgrade, however the Red Cross had not paid for his services and he was supported by the Quakers while he worked for them, so he did not complain. In late July 1919 he went to London to sign up.

Allen was one of a number of Australian men who did not care to return to their lives and wives in Australia. They were prepared to stay behind in Europe, serving in some military capacity as long as they could. Some had good reason not to return to their old lives. The horrible disfigurement they had suffered during the war was one of the reasons. Having become amputees, these soldiers felt they would be a burden to their families if they returned. Some men had started new lives in either England or France, marrying a new wife and abandoning the old one. By the end of 1920 an increasing number of women, having never received word that their husbands had died in battle or been reported as missing in action, were wondering where their husbands had gone. One of them was Lena Lear, who was looking for her husband, John Henry Lear, who had served in the 3rd Light Horse Brigade. At the end of the war John had sought assistance from the Repatriation Department in Melbourne but he had never come home.[7]

Wives began inquiring at the War Office in Melbourne about the whereabouts of their spouses, but unless abandonment had taken place before the discharge of the soldier involved, there was nothing the military was either willing or able to do. If the soldier had been officially discharged from the army then he no longer came under the responsibility of the AIF, so in most cases the women and their children were left to fend for themselves.[8]

In London Allen was briefed about his new job. It would not be easy, Hobbs had assured him, because the AGS was in the process of establishing itself and it would be a challenging task to help mould it. Halfway through 1919, Allen left for

France accompanied by General Hobbs, who wanted to explain to him the work in progress on site. Trusting Allen's expertise as an architect, Hobbs thought it advisable to hand all the constructional matters over to the Australian.

When Allen informed Captain Spedding that he would from now on take over the construction of the monuments, Spedding reacted as if stung by a bee and absolutely refused to acknowledge Allen's position. Spedding let Allen know that he had hired a French constructor and that there were contracts in place—contracts that couldn't just be terminated. Spedding had hired stonemasons, the Devereaux brothers, to do the work and, as far as he was concerned, they would continue to do it.[9]

This became a matter of dispute between Spedding and Allen. Hobbs had personally appointed Allen for the construction work and Allen considered it his special duty to plan the five monuments that were to be erected. He asked for the plans for the monuments that the Devereaux brothers had completed but he never got them. A number of requests to have them sent to him were ignored and, when he was finally able to inspect what the brothers had built, he found the monuments incomplete.

As head of construction, Allen refused to accept them in their current unfinished state. He wrote to headquarters, advising them to retain an amount of money before paying the bill. But he was too late to stop the payments—the amount of 700 pounds had already been paid. It was a waste of money, Allen claimed.[10]

In an attempt to find an ally to help solve the construction problems, Allen thought of approaching Captain Barden, who was responsible for negotiating with the landowners to secure the sites for the Australian battle memorials. Barden had little knowledge of the French language, so Lieutenant Hillton usually accompanied him on his travels and acted as his interpreter. Both men were stationed at Villers-Bretonneux.

Before Allen actually contacted Barden, he learned that both Barden and Hillton worked outside the AGS and were AIF men. It was Allen's experience that soldiers teamed together and did not look too favourably on someone not from the military. Allen later told Hobbs that when he visited Villers-Bretonneux and ran into Barden and Hillton, both men had ignored him.

Allen also complained that no officer ever visited Poperinghe during those first months. Although his work was proceeding well, he was left pretty much to fend for himself. Spedding, his superior officer at the time, would travel to Amiens a few times a month, but he would never drop by at Poperinghe. Allen felt 'all were against me'.[11] One of his drivers had overheard Spedding talking to an officer at Amiens. Spedding had said that although Allen worked hard, he thought the major would have to go.

Not having a military background and not being familiar with its procedures made Allen's appointment a questionable one for the men who had come from the military. Allen was aware that he was not well liked and he often felt ignored by the other men in the AGS in France. On top of that, he had to deal with Lee and Kingston, who were constantly at each other's throats and did not speak directly to each other. It was becoming ridiculous and almost impossible to do the work, so he returned to London in February 1920 to take up matters with General Hobbs.

In London Allen met Major Phillips for the first time. Spedding apparently had left somewhat unexpectedly at the start of the new year and Phillips introduced himself as his new OC. Allen immediately took a shine to the fellow. Phillips had been in charge of Lewes Barracks; although his superiors had been very satisfied with Phillips' work at Lewes, Allen knew well enough how the soldiers regarded anyone connected with the military police. Phillips would not have made many friends in this line of work; like Allen himself, he was an outcast. Phillips said that he hoped to be able to work together with Allen in the near future. This was exactly what Allen wanted to hear—they could now tackle the problems in France together.

Explaining the situation in France to Hobbs and Phillips that morning, Allen made it clear that either Kingston or Lee would need to go. He was tired of Lee's chronic complaints and described Lee's antagonism toward Kingston as a 'mental craze'.[12] He let Hobbs know that there was a dire need in France for one officer in charge of controlling all the areas. Having one officer who resided in London most of the time as the only OC just did not work, Allen complained. There was a need for an officer on the ground, someone who had the authority to intervene when needed, to discipline and supervise the men. Allen returned to France as inspector of the graves services and, together with Major Phillips as OC in London, they would become responsible for the AGS.

Because he spoke a little French and Flemish, Allen had been stationed in Belgium. Allen's office and staff had settled at Bird Cage Camp in the small town of Poperinghe on the

French–Belgian border. Bird Cage Camp was no Valhalla. The huts were basic and hard to keep warm, but Allen had experienced worse places. At Gouda the accommodation had heating, but it was very simple. There had been no luxury in the camp, but his life as a Quaker had prepared him for asceticism; he had no desire for opulence. His men could often be heard complaining about the very basic accommodation at Bird Cage, but Allen never whined about it. Those who visited the camp always commented on Allen's good humour and spirited personality. Although some found it strange that the small town of Poperinghe—with its many bars, prostitutes and distilleries—appealed to Allen so much.

During the war Poperinghe had become a popular place for the soldiers to take a break from the fighting. With about 11,000 inhabitants it was not a small village and had enough amenities to amuse a large population of mainly British and Australian soldiers. Most of the town's children and been sent to Rouen or Paris when the fighting began, as thousands of soldiers stayed or passed through the town on a daily basis. It was referred to as the 'British back front area', the first stop-off after hell, a getaway from the madness of the trenches. At one time there were as many as 40,000 soldiers making their way into the town and, at the height of the war, the residents counted 72 train carriages filled with soldiers arriving daily from the front. The soldiers sometimes found a room with the locals but were mainly housed in tents at the town's borders. As the war continued and winter conditions made living in a tent impossible, the tents were gradually replaced by barracks.

The town's position, just before the engagement lines, made it a perfect haven—it was close enough to the front line to be directly accessible for the wounded and the weary, but not so near as to be positively bombed to ruins. It became a magnet for the soldiers not because of its merits but through logic and its location. 'Pops', as the men called it, became a well-liked destination.[13]

Unlike Villers-Bretonneux, Amiens and all those other towns, it had not suffered devastation; on the contrary, 'Pops' had flourished. Belgium did not produce any wheat and had historically been reliant on German imports for most of its food needs, so at the beginning of the war, when Germany became the enemy and stopped exporting its products, a food shortage hit Belgium. Because Belgium towns became a gathering place for their soldiers, the British stepped in to help the small country and sent relief food across the channel. Some eighty thousand tonnes of flour poured into Poperinghe at the beginning of the war. The town never experienced a food problem after that and survived the war without hunger.

The locals had gone about their daily routines during the war and, when thousands of soldiers spent their wages in the town, looking for a shave, amusement and a drink, the residents made a bit of money on the side. In the fields around the town the Belgian farmers produced hops and distilleries were set up all over town (even in backyards), so there was beer and whisky in abundance to satisfy the thirsty hordes of soldiers. And with prostitutes flocking to the town to entertain them, 'Pops' became an adult playground. With all of this activity, most of its residents came out of the war much wealthier than they had entered it.

The small town also had a beautiful ambience, with its iconic town hall, churches, cobbled streets and charming little houses. Alfred Allen could live there happily, even if it meant living in a sober wooden hut. But after he had established his headquarters, he began to feel it was time that his duties as supreme authority in France were put into practice.

Chapter 8
THE UGLY JOB

When AIF headquarters in London received Willoughby Bollen's letter, they could hardly believe his allegations were directed at the officer in charge at Villers-Bretonneux. They might have dismissed his accusations if Bollen had been the only person who had sent them such a letter—but he wasn't. A number of other men also complained about the behaviour of officers working for the AGS. Most of the allegations were against Charles Kingston, a man who had barely a year prior been rewarded for his bravery with a DCM, but complaints were also made against Alfred Allen. At AIF headquarters on Horseferry Road they wondered how this could have happened. What was going on across the Channel?

Rose Venn-Brown had a fair idea of what the problem was. She was one of the first women to be taken on by the Australian Graves Services at the beginning of 1919.[1] Understanding the need for help in those first years of the war, she travelled to

Europe from Sydney's Lane Cove in January 1915 and joined the Red Cross, spending much of the war distributing Australian comforts from the Red Cross post at Le Havre. As well as her Red Cross activities, Rose also became the entertainment supervisor at the YMCA. She was a great piano player and something of an entertainer, but she was also deeply aware of the need for families back home to know where missing relatives were buried.

After the Armistice, she was called to London where she was immediately appointed to the medical records at Horseferry Road. A few months later she was asked to go to work for the AGS.

Rose Venn-Brown would often be the first person to open and read the pleading letters coming in from Australia, grieving mothers and wives who longed for a sign or a photograph—anything that could take away the desolate feeling that people have when a loved one 'disappears'. They would almost beg her to locate the whereabouts of their relatives' bodies. She began touring the devastated areas, collecting photographs of graves.[2] At Abbeville graveyard she noted the name of every single Australian buried there and took photographs of the cemetery and the graves. In May 1919, she sent the list and the photographs to her mother in Sydney asking her to forward them to newspapers to be published. The response from the Australian people was overwhelming and even Rose was surprised by the many letters of thanks she received from relatives.

Rose had a very feminine approach to tending the graves and spent hours planting poppies or forget-me-nots in an attempt to bring warmth and colour to the graveyards that were scattered across that dark and battered landscape. She was also aware that even the beauty of the flowers could not take away her knowledge of the unspeakable truth they covered. Returning from France to London, she told people: 'The more beautiful the flowers are, the worse it is underfoot.'[3]

After spending months in Villers-Bretonneux Rose knew how difficult it must be for the soldiers left behind to scour the countryside searching for comrades. Bodies, often buried by shellfire or swallowed by mud, would have to be pulled from the clinging earth, sometimes in pieces. Those doing the digging even stood a chance of losing their own lives when shovelling for a body. She had seen soldiers take a deep breath as the sound of metal on metal came from the earth, knowing they might set off a grenade or bomb. When no discharge followed she'd heard them release their breath in thankful, anxious gasps.

She knew that many soldiers drank, though not all of them. She'd come across those who misbehaved, and although she found their conduct unacceptable, she could nevertheless understand their need to find an outlet in mischief.

Rose lived in Villers-Bretonneux for most of 1919 and was acquainted with Charlie Kingston. Yes, Kingston would drink with his men, she told them at Horseferry Road, even she had groped for a bottle now and again. 'You have no idea what it's like,' she said about Villers-Bretonneux. 'It was like living in a graveyard.'[4] The terrible silence and sadness of the battlegrounds after the living had gone made her feel so depressed at times that she could hardly speak. She had found it hard to proceed with the work she was doing; the evenings, when she provided some entertainment for the men playing her piano, she found the most difficult. She was always glad to return to London, where civilisation had not ceased to exist.

Everyone realised the work wasn't pretty. It took a certain type of individual to be able to stomach it. After the English located an Australian body, the AIF clearance crew would come in and the discovered remains would have to be placed on cresol-soaked canvas. A careful examination had to be made of the pockets, neck, wrists and trouser braces for identification tags. The men in the graves services would sometimes need to wade into a heap of mangled bodies. The bodies then had to be bagged and loaded onto a truck, to be moved to an appropriate cemetery where they would be reburied.

The stories told by men who had served in the AGS were horrific. Young men who had survived the horrors of war and subsequently volunteered for the AGS, in an effort to do something for their slain comrades, almost lost their minds after months of dragging what one man called 'bags of slime from the mud of Flanders'. Lifting a body from the earth with a shovel while some of its parts fell back into the mud had brought home to them very graphically the ugly reality of death.

Wil McBeath, who served in the AGS in France, wrote home to his mother that as he was digging up a body he realised it was the corpse of his mate Richie Nicolls. McBeath made no secret that he hated the work: 'I can't say I'm in love with the job. Digging up the bodies is the easiest but I'd rather be in the cemetery digging the graves. It's terribly hard ground but it's a clean job.'⁵ In his letters home he admitted that the effects of doing such a job became evident in the men's behaviour within weeks. Drinking, fighting, going on strike and even looting a body were not uncommon practices.

The work was almost too much to ask from any person, but all involved realised the importance of finding the corpses in order to give the families of the dead some kind of closure. The people at home needed to know that their loved ones were laid to rest in decent graves—graves they could one day visit or at least imagine visiting. A place to grieve. This wasn't a job for the weak-hearted.

At Horseferry Road, the initial reaction to the accusations being made was shock and disbelief. When they phoned the continent and inquired further, they were told by Kingston that both Lee and Bollen were grumblers and not up to the job. That was why they were being sent back to England to be demobilised.

A Lieutenant Colonel D.R. Osborne wrote a letter to Lee saying that he had made investigations and that it appeared there was some truth to Lee's grievances. Lee had sent the AIF a letter from the mayor of Villers-Bretonneux, plus a letter written by a group of ladies from the town who were most upset about the behaviour of the Australian men living in huts on the grounds of the 'Red Chateau'. If it were all true then it was a very serious situation and the AIF could not just let it pass by. They would need to take some kind of action.

Now that Bollen had revealed specific deficiencies in the AGS—its dysfunctional leadership, and especially the allegation that certain members of the services in Villers-Bretonneux and

Amiens were bringing the good name of the AIF into disrepute—something needed to be done. Weeding out those responsible and removing the disturbing influences would be an inevitable precautionary measure. Any form of punishment would need to be carefully determined and dealt with.

The commanding officer of the AIF in London at this time, Lieutenant Colonel Alfred Jackson, suggested to the high commissioner that a court of inquiry be held. Jackson was an old boy of Melbourne Grammar School who had started his military career in 1914 as a captain. He had left Australia for Egypt with the 58th Regiment, known as the Essendon Regiment, and had been given a commission in the 7th Battalion, where he was quickly promoted to major. Wounded at Gallipoli, after his recovery he was sent to France where he was promoted to lieutenant colonel. In March 1919, his name was gazetted as having been brought to the notice of the secretary of state for war 'for valuable services rendered in connection with the war' and he was awarded the Order of the British Empire.[6] He was a highly respected officer.

All agreed that holding a classified inquiry would be the best course of action to take. The inquiry's panel would require members who were fully authorised to investigate the alleged grievances and allegations, and this would preferably need to happen before things got entirely out of hand. The AIF would try to keep matters confidential by calling up witnesses at the last moment; by keeping the public and any journalists out of the equation, the proceedings could be monitored without attracting undesirable attention. The inquiry would be held in

France, far away from the nosey newspapers reporters and the public eye. It was also where most of the people involved were residing and could be questioned.

To head the inquiry, three men were picked who were all attached to the AIF. The president and highest in rank was Alan Lloyd MacLean. He was 39 years old, held the title of honorary major and was a draftsman by trade. Suffering from attacks of muscular rheumatism, he wasn't a well man by any means. He had recently had all his teeth pulled because they were causing him a lot of pain, but his gums had subsequently become infected and as a result he wished he hadn't. He was still tormented by pain on a daily basis.

MacLean was pursuing a municipal course in engineering at Manchester University; AIF men could apply for a course there while they waited to be demobilised and many took the free courses offered to them because this provided them with a steady income from the military until they had finished their studies.

The second member of the court was Captain William Thomas Meikle, 35, a motor mechanic who had served in Egypt and had suffered a bout of typhoid fever in 1916. Sent back to Australia to recover, he married Dorothy Blanchard in 1917 but his health remained cause for concern for a long time. After the Armistice he was recalled to London to serve the AIF as an administrator. On his many visits to London, Allen often sought the company of Meikle as well as that of the third member of the court.

That member was Captain Philip Fennelly. Although the papers establishing the court of inquiry stated that all three men had some kind of legal background, this was only actually true in Fennelly's case. A bachelor of 44 years of age, he had been a barrister back in Sydney. He had also attended the same school as George Phillips. They had known each other for years and both had served in the 3rd Pioneer Battalion.

Realising that their men had turned on them and that they too were being accused of certain irregularities including conspiracy, bad leadership and maladministration, both Phillips and Allen were pleased to have friends hearing the inquiry. Lee also claimed that Phillips had unjustly relieved him of his duties with the intention of filling his vacancy with someone from the military police. During the proceedings, Phillips and Allen were not only allowed to attend the inquiry but also to cross-examine all the witnesses. The witnesses, called up one by one, felt that the procedure was anything but impartial.

Those called to testify found it difficult being interrogated by the very people they had accused, as well as by the president and the two other members of the court. Called up separately on different days, without any prior warning, none of them was even aware that an inquiry was taking place until they were seated in the witness chair.

In Villers-Bretonneux on 30 March 1920, the inquiry began into certain allegations of misconduct by men attached to the AGS. It would last ten days.

Chapter 9
THE INQUIRY IN FRANCE
30 March 1920

The inquiry started on 30 March with Captain Kingston as the first witness. Appointed to the AGD on 25 August 1919, his principal duties were the charge, control and management of the photographic and transport sections at Villers-Bretonneux. A month after his appointment the organisation of the Australian Graves Services in France came into effect.

There was no actual coordination between the various sectors and each officer acted independently, reporting direct to Australia House in London. After the men had been forced to leave the chateau and had erected huts on the grounds it soon become apparent that their quarters at Villers-Bretonneux were poorly constructed and badly ventilated and were, in fact, totally unfit to live in. Sometimes the men lived in these huts together with their wives.

The administration at Villers-Bretonneux was also a shambles. No record was kept of any leave granted, so the men tended to come and go as they pleased. Leave passes, signed in blank, were left with a non-commissioned officer for distribution. No books were properly kept and motor transport equipment, stores or petrol could be acquired without any approval from an officer.[1] Needless to say, abuse was widespread. The issuing of petrol was random and equally unsupervised. Drivers were at liberty to help themselves, which they did, often selling or distributing petrol to the people of Villers-Bretonneux.[2] Members of staff visiting adjacent towns to go to a bar or a brothel used cars intended for the transport section to get them there. Drunkenness was common and on some occasions, when men came back to camp after a night out, they were known to discharge their guns on their way to their huts.[3]

The men slept in the huts on the chateau grounds, but a couple of them were staying at different estaminets in the village. There had not been sufficient accommodation on the chateau grounds at the time, Kingston testified.

The photographers were very unproductive during the winter of 1919–20. On average, the twelve men at Villers-Bretonneux posted for this task would produce about four photos a day between them. This drove up the cost of a photograph to about fifteen shillings each. Kingston and his men justified this by claiming that the weather had made work almost impossible—it was either too wet or too cold—and at times transportation was also a problem. There were working parties who got their verbal orders on very short notice, sometimes on the evening before the work was to be done. The next morning these parties would travel up to a hundred miles to get to a certain location. They would use motor cars or the ambulance stationed at Villers-Bretonneux to get from one location to another, but at times the cars were in use elsewhere or had maintenance problems.

Kingston did not deny that his men, especially during the winter months, sometimes sat around doing nothing for weeks on end and that he had made no arrangements to employ them in some other capacity. The result of all this was that they lay about the camp or wandered about in the neighbouring villages and towns with nothing to do for months.

These bored men became very resourceful when it came to making a pound on the side. Thomas William MacKay was placed under open arrest for trying to sell an ambulance to a man in Rouen. Every now and then a car would be mysteriously 'lost'. Kingston told the court that he had no guard for the cars stationed in the garage on the chateau grounds.[4] After use, cars were simply left in the shed without any form of lock-up or guard to watch over them. Stealing a vehicle was relatively simple.

The men involved in 'losing' a car worked as a team.[5] One man would drive the vehicle to a designated spot, where an accomplice would 'steal' the car and drive it to Calais. An Englishman in league with a ship's officer and also an army officer in Rouen were in on the scam. After the ship's officer drew up the papers, the car would be loaded onto the ship crossing the Channel. Once shipped off to England, the driver would report the car as being 'lost or stolen'. The vehicle would land in England with its papers in place and without anyone knowing it had been nicked. Corporal MacKay worked together with Wally Furby, one of the drivers. Furby was responsible for registering the car as stolen and he was also the person responsible for drawing up a report about the theft.[6]

In the beginning Furby had been apprehensive about the whole affair, but MacKay had explained to him that this swindle involved hardly any risk. As they sat drinking a coffee with rum in a small bar, MacKay managed to persuade Furby to come aboard, assuring him that it was not the first time he had been involved in the swindle and that it had already proved successful on quite a number of occasions. A car would fetch up to twenty thousand francs, he told Furby, and the proceeds were divided equally between the men involved.[7] As this story unfolded, the court members could only stare in disbelief at what they were hearing from the witnesses who were called up one by one.

Rations, available in abundance, were managed by the British and issued to the officer in charge—in this case, Kingston. The food and drink were collected at the Mericourt supply dump.[8] Because of the abundance of food, everyone ate on the chateau grounds. Although not in accordance with the rules, the wives all used the sergeants' mess and thus enjoyed free meals. Local women who stayed the night, and were probably involved in prostitution, would also eat there. Major Allen used the mess when he visited and all the British exhumation parties enjoyed meals there when they worked in the neighbourhood. Drinks were served and it was all free. No one paid for their own food, yet everyone appeared to be on a sustenance allowance.

The supply depot—where clothes, utensils and goods such as toothpaste, shaving cream and household needs were stored— was located in the basement of the chateau, where Madame

Delacour had allowed the use of the cellar. It was supposed to be administrated by the quartermaster Charles Leary.[9] Being the quartermaster was not Leary's official duty; he was actually in charge of the memorial cross party, but he also kept an occasional record of the stores. The quartermaster was put in charge of the key to the stores but he didn't make a fuss if anyone needed something from the depot. He simply gave them the key.

The petrol dump was located in one of the sheds on the chateau grounds. If a man needed petrol, he could take whatever he needed; although he was supposed to note it in the logbook, the men rarely did so and no one questioned the quantity of petrol drawn. Petrol wasn't measured out in any way because nobody had been given responsibility for its distribution. It was left to the drivers' own judgement how much they would need and how much they would withdraw from the dump.

As the hearing wore on, it became evident that some men had been involved in a swindle involving tyres and other spare parts held at the base depot at Rouen. The illustrious Wally Furby and Corporal MacKay also happened to be the culprits in this scam. The base depot in Rouen was an easy target when it came to forged orders.[10]

MacKay would forge an order for tyres and other spare parts, which he would hand over to the quartermaster in Rouen, who would then supply them with the parts they needed. Furby and MacKay would stuff the tyres and various other auto parts into the ambulance they always used to pick up stores in and would drive it to a garage at Villers-Bretonneux. Unloading the loot, they sold it all to the owner, who gave a good price. Auto parts and tyres were at that time almost impossible to get hold of, so the business was very lucrative.

The signature on the order for the tyres turned out to be Kingston's, but he denied any knowledge of the scam. He did confess to the court that he had given MacKay some signed blank orders when he sent him to Calais to pick up stores and provisions, on the basis that it would be quicker for both of them if MacKay could fill in the forms himself. It went without saying that Kingston fully trusted MacKay and was very surprised to hear the man had betrayed his trust.

Kingston had never been aware of the swindle, he testified, nor had he been approached by the people responsible for it in Rouen. MacKay explained to the court that it had all been quite easy. There was no counterfoil on the use of blanks, so no distributer got a receipt, and, if the original order was destroyed, it would have been very difficult to keep track of any supplies going out.

Sometime later, Kingston, realising that Leary was not appropriately keeping track of the supplies, put MacKay in charge of maintaining the inventory of the stores.[11] MacKay had been stupefied and couldn't believe his luck. Now in full control of supplies, he could really exploit his talents. It was only a matter of time before everyone knew that MacKay would write up his inventory 'lightly'. This meant he would write up his stock as being 'short' on certain articles, and he was known to have made as many as fifty tyres disappear in this way. No one complained because everyone involved profited from it.

One day Kingston reported the loss of an ambulance, destroyed by fire. The ambulance had been loaded with supplies, such as boots, clothing and cookers, and was stolen after coming off the boat at Calais.[12] It was never found at that time, but Kingston later reported that his men had found its burnt-out wreck in a field. Kingston told the court that he had reported the whole incident to Allen, who had made a personal inquiry into the matter but Kingston had not heard what had happened as a result of that inquiry. When items allegedly lost in the 'fire' started showing up on the streets of Villers-Bretonneux, suspicion arose. Suddenly French men were seen walking around in Australian army boots and women were selling chestnuts roasted on the Tommy burners that had gone missing in the fire.

Kingston testified that he himself had reprimanded the men who were responsible. Kingston told the court that he had given Allen full details about what was going on at Villers-Bretonneux. On Allen's various visits, Kingston had also let him know that he had taken disciplinary actions against those responsible.

Earlier on, when Captain Spedding was still OC in London, Kingston had complained about the behaviour of his men, he said. Spedding had reacted by sending instructions for him to demobilise the men who behaved unacceptably. No surprise that he set to this task vigorously, weeding out the men he did not like.[13] The AIF then started complaining about the numbers of men being sent to London for demobilisation. Demobilising them was no hardship; the problem was that Kingston requested to have them replaced by others. Fed up with the extra work

Kingston was creating, the AIF told him to stop this practice immediately, which he did.

Fennelly, Meikle and MacLean were also informed about the various men who ran estaminets, acted as pimps for the women they were living with and wore their Australian uniform in the process. These disgraces had mostly taken place in Villers-Bretonneux, which was under the command of Distinguished Medal possessor Charles Kingston.

Contrary to what Kingston claimed, the court found he had actually done very little to discipline his men; in fact, he appeared to be an accessory to some of their behaviour and crimes. To make it all even worse, the men who had now got wind of the allegations against Kingston had drawn up a petition in his favour. Fearing that Lee, who was not well liked, would take his place if Kingston was removed, they praised Kingston's ability to lead them and lauded him for his qualities as the OC of the photographic and motorised sections at Villers-Bretonneux. They managed to gather signatures from all three districts, Villers, Amiens and Poperinghe. Almost all the men had signed their names to the paper in his favour. The members of the court were disgusted with the petition and disregarded it when it appeared at the hearing.

While a number of drivers gave their testimony after Kingston, Major MacLean fidgeted his way through the hearings. In constant pain and not feeling at all well, he patiently listened as these drivers explained how Bollen had rubbed them up the wrong way. They claimed that the man was a constant grumbler, and accused him and his wife of being overly friendly with the

German prisoners in the camp. A couple of Germans had been seen entering Bollen's hut in the evenings and they sometimes stayed for hours. The men could only guess at what was going on, but they suspected the Bollens and the 'Boche' were up to no good.[14]

Willoughby Bollen, when he was called up to testify, did not deny having friendly relationships with the prisoners. He had been suffering from a boil on his face, he explained, and the Germans were the only ones who had shown any sympathy. They had more than once cleaned the infected areas and bandaged them.

As accusations, suspicions and misgivings mounted, it became clear to the court that the Australian Graves Services had suffered severely in the past from lack of organisation and supervision. The members of the panel feared the consequences if this matter ever found its way out of the confines of the court and became common knowledge. The culprits formed a relatively small section of the AGS and the hope was that they would not go public.

Divided into three distinct sections, with one chief inspector who appeared to have little or no authority, the situation had been bound to get out of hand at some point. High Commissioner Fisher, who should have intervened immediately, was at that stage on the verge of a nervous breakdown; he had tried desperately, as the accusations mounted, to sweep the whole matter under the carpet.

Depriving Allen of any authority had been the doing of Captain Spedding; this was something that Fisher, as the person with supreme responsibility, should have taken note of.

Spedding had made it clear that Allen was not to interfere in the other districts. This would not have been a very workable situation for Allen, the members of the court—who were also to some extent Allen's friends—thought.

Chapter 10
THE COURT IN LONDON
6 April 1920

It was not long before a rumour spread in France that there was something going on. After a number of men had given testimony, a whisper began meandering through the ranks. It was claimed that the presiding officer, Alan MacLean, had openly boasted that, after the key witnesses were eradicated from the AGS, he and Captain Meikle would be appointed to the vacant positions. If true this meant that the members on the inquiry were being bribed.

Fennelly was very much aware of MacLean's desire to obtain a position with the AGS. MacLean had approached him about this personally and confided that he had sufficient influence to secure such a position.[1] He had in fact been promised such a position but did not reveal who had made the promise.

Fennelly went to Phillips wanting to know if this was true and what it was all about, but Phillips denied having any knowledge of it and stressed that he had certainly not promised the man a position with the AGS. Fennelly left it at that. Phillips was his friend and he had no reason to doubt his word. But the rumour had got around and became a persistent subject of gossip at AIF headquarters in London. In fact, at some point everyone in the office appeared to be talking or making jokes about it.

Lieutenant Colonel Jackson, having got wind of the matter, set out to put a stop to it. He spoke to High Commissioner Fisher and requested Fennelly to return to London. Jackson told Fennelly that he no longer wished for MacLean to be a member of the court—he would have to be removed, if only to avoid any suspicion of a miscarriage of justice. Jackson made it clear that he wanted the man returned to Australia as soon as possible.

MacLean was very anxious to stay in London, however, and he loudly protested against Jackson's decision. But the colonel had clearly made up his mind. MacLean was shipped back to Australia, boarding the HMAT *Hororata* two days later.[2] On arrival in Australia, Captain MacLean claimed that his physical incapacity had prevented him from continuing with the hearing, which might have been partially true.

Fisher found it advisable to hold the remainder of the hearings in London, under AIF supervision. So, on 6 April, the court of inquiry was relocated to England, at AIF headquarters on Horseferry Road. Captain Fennelly was now the president and Captain Meikle the only other member.

On 26 March Allen and Phillips told William Lee he had been suspended because of incompetence and he was to return to England. Arriving in London on 28 March, Lee heard that an inquiry addressing the problems in France was already in progress and he was more than eager to testify. He could tell them a thing or two. Finally, on 7 April, Lee gave his testimony in London, although he had not been told until the day before that this would be required of him.

At AIF headquarters, they already knew about Lee's complaints; he had written them down in a rather rambling letter.[3] The animosity between Lee and Kingston had obviously originated from a disagreement about how and where wages were paid, as Lee especially vented his frustration about the fact that the salaries were distributed at a local bar in Amiens.

But Kingston appeared to be not the only person who had rubbed William Lee up the wrong way; he had also drawn up a list of complaints and questions concerning Major Allen. Lee accused him of selling Australian Red Cross comforts to the English and French people. Three hundred cases of comforts, such as cigarettes, shaving utensils, biscuits, blankets, clothing and cooking appliances, meant for the Australians and addressed to Major Alfred Allen by the Red Cross, had gone mysteriously missing. Lee had noticed how a number of these items had suddenly turned up among the residents of Villers-Bretonneux.

As far as Lee was concerned, Allen was slack. The major had not done anything to address the irregularities Lee had brought to his attention, including the behaviour of men like Kingston, but also disturbing mistakes such as crosses bearing wrong names and being placed over random graves. Lee claimed the general condition of the memorials was appalling and that Allen, as the special officer in charge of the memorials, should have taken appropriate action. Lee had reported all this to Australia House as well as to Allen. The work of restoring and preserving the graves was being carelessly and inefficiently carried out, so much so that Lee had become ashamed of his uniform. To Lee, Villers-Bretonneux was a sacred place and he felt ashamed that the AGS had done more to degrade their uniform there than any other unit in France.[4] He stated all of this firmly to the members of the court.

As a last resort, Lee had approached the British military police after witnessing terrible misconduct by the men, but they had told him the Australians were out of their jurisdiction. The idea had arisen that the men in the AGS were beyond the reach of any military discipline, because most of them were in the process of being discharged from the AIF and were either being sent home or being re-employed by the AGS as civilians.

The court listened patiently to Lee but, when it was time to question the witness, both Fennelly and Phillips revealed that Lee was by no means squeaky clean. Lee admitted that he was living in Amiens with a woman who was not his wife, but he saw no harm in this at all. The woman's name was Madame Legion and Lee claimed she was his housekeeper and taking her to bed with him was, in Lee's opinion, 'a condition necessary to a man's life'.[5] After all, his wife lived in Australia and he did not believe in celibacy.

Lee then became indignant, because this line of questioning had suddenly turned him into a suspect instead of a witness. The people he had accused were the ones who should be interrogated since he was not the only one making complaints against them. The people of Villers-Bretonneux had vented their disgust about the manner in which the Australians conducted themselves in a letter.

On 19 March, Lee had received an anonymous letter from 'the concerned women of Villers-Bretonneux'.[6] The letter, written in French, made it clear that the women were appalled by the conduct of the Australians in their town. It went on to describe how a fire had started at the lodgings situated in the gardens of Madame Delacour, where the Australians were living, and how half a dozen naked girls had been seen running out of the lodgings. It was scandalous, they wrote, and if such a thing ever happened again they would be forced to inform the French military authorities. They needed to protect their children, especially young girls, from witnessing such undesirable behaviour.

Lee also produced a letter from the mayor of Villers-Bretonneux that he had received on 23 March.[7] The mayor, Dr Vaudeville, declared that it was common knowledge that women of ill repute were living in the Australian soldiers' barracks at Villers-Bretonneux, sharing their lives with the soldiers. The mayor went on to write that if the Australian soldiers were under any kind of military control, the women would have to go. The current situation was a terrible example for the population living in the area. A month ago, the mayor had received a denunciation from an anonymous source, which he forwarded to the French police.

Bitter and angry that his appointment at the AGS had been suspended, Lee had handed over all the letters of complaint he had received to Australia House on the day he arrived from France, among them a letter from Lieutenant Colonel Osborne.

But the court became suspicious about the authenticity of Lee's letters; no one knew a Lieutenant Colonel Osborne. He was not registered with the Australian Army and Fennelly and Meikle wondered where he had come from. Lee could not answer their questions. He told the court that Osborne was an Australian serving in the British Army.[8] The members of the court also requested a sample of Lee's French girlfriend's handwriting. The letter sent to the court from France proved to be remarkably similar to that in the letter from the anonymous female villagers.

After further questioning by the court, Lee admitted that Dr Vaudeville's letter had been written at Lee's request and in his presence. Lee had also authorised Osborne's letter. The watermark on all the letters showed they had been written on English Red Cross paper, and there was some suggestion that Lee might have supplied and even supervised the accusations. The letters went out of their way to stress that Lee himself was not to blame for any of the problems in France.

During questioning, it became clear that Lee's men were, just like Kingston's men, in the business of running estaminets. One of Lee's men had been reported serving drinks while in uniform. There was so much going on that Lee began to regret having put himself on the stand—the hearing was turning against him. He had come forward because of a quarrel and yet quickly he was becoming one of the accused.

When it was time for Alfred Allen to take the stand, he immediately let the court know that he did not find Lee's presence in Amiens essential. If the staff and workforce there came under his control, he could easily supervise the work together with Sergeant Black, who had been stationed in Amiens for a long time and who Allen knew as a good and reliable man. He would be able to count on Black to take over the supervision of the area from him when Allen returned to Poperinghe.

In Belgium Allen had been supplied with a draftsman, a clerk and a driver. He was also in charge of five photographers. Allen told the court that, besides their photographic work, they also performed various other tasks, such as helping with the maintenance of the cars and maintaining the Australian graves in the cemeteries. These extra responsibilities were mostly meant to keep the men busy when the weather conditions did not permit using a camera. Quakers did not appreciate lethargy.

Allen explained that he felt seriously understaffed when it came to checking the particulars on graves. He himself had found numerous mistakes made when it came to the names on crosses and the locations they were supposed to be found. He would certainly like to have more able men available for him to deploy in the field.

Allen considered having a draftsman an absolute waste of money.[9] The man was only there to draw up the plans for a cemetery when the original plans with the names of the Australians buried there could not be obtained from Winchester House in London, where the office of the director of Graves Registration and Enquiries had been located during the war. Now it held all the blueprints for the cemeteries and would draw up new ones once the coordinates were passed on to their architects. Besides, Allen was an architect himself and could easily take over the work of the draftsman.

Allen let the court know that if the men on his photographic team could be employed only to take photos then he would be able to cut their numbers down from five to three. Strangely, although the job did not call for it, Allen had promoted them all to sergeants. When asked about this, he explained that he had done this very deliberately. Giving them an officer's rank contributed to their wellbeing and willingness to do the job at hand with devotion. It gave them a sense of status and this rubbed off on their work. Of course, it also meant that they were paid higher wages. It made the major a popular boss and Allen did not deny it.

Allen complained to the court that he had nothing to say when it came to disciplining his men in Poperinghe, because he had orders from Australia House that this particular aspect of their control fell under the supervision of Kingston.

When questioned about the animosity between Lee and Kingston, Allen said he thought it might have originated when Kingston had been awarded the rank of captain and Lee, who had a similar job, was left a lieutenant. The whole matter, Allen thought, had been fed by jealousy from the start. Lee complained constantly about Kingston but, when Allen looked into it, he found nothing to support the allegations made by Lee.

Kingston too had complained about Lee, but in this instance also Allen had found nothing to back the man's misgivings. Allen told the court that he had not noted excessive drinking when he visited either Amiens or Villers-Bretonneux and the only cases of immorality he had heard about were those presented before the court that day. Although he visited regularly, he was adamant that he had not noticed any wrongdoings.

Allen went on to advise the court to centralise the work in France, preferably placing its headquarters in Poperinghe. It would be the most logical place to have a control centre because the greater part of the work that needed to be done was undoubtedly in the northern sector.

In the meantime, Lee had requested to be heard by the court a second time. There were a number of questions he wanted to ask at a second hearing. When he had first been called, he had felt caught out because of the very short notice he had been given. He claimed that he had not been able to prepare his testimony as well as he would have wanted to.

The questions he wanted answered all concerned Allen and his position in the AGS.[10] Lee was disgusted that the major had taken up an AIF appointment only after the war had ended and he wanted Allen to explain why he had refused to do his bit while the fighting was going on. He suspected him of having business interests in Europe—interests that no doubt interfered with his job at the AGS. Allen's visits across the Channel to England were frequent and Lee doubted that they were all a result of his work at the AGS; he wondered if the AGS was aware of all these visits.

Lee knew that Allen's female driver had at one time gone to England on leave and had subsequently stayed away for weeks. She had been employed by the Red Cross to assist Allen and Lee wanted to know if Allen had taken measures to prevent her staying away for weeks on end. Lee also knew of other cases where Allen's men left their posts for extended periods. He wanted the matter looked into.

During their very first meeting, Lee had showed Allen a map and had pointed out the different gravesites on it. Allen, Lee claimed, had seemed confused when Lee told him the coordinates; it was then that Lee realised that the man appeared to have no knowledge of map reading whatsoever.

Lee had recorded an instance when Allen had made a request to the Red Cross for three hundred parcels of comforts to be delivered to him personally, and he doubted that Allen made it known to the Red Cross that he was not in fact the OC of the AGS. It had been rumoured that an inquiry in London was made into lost Red Cross reliefs and that Allen had been called to testify. Certain members of his staff had been sent to prison as a result, but Allen had come through the inquiry unscathed. The major had insinuated more than once that he would one day take complete control of the AGS. Allen was a wolf in sheep's clothing, said Lee, who added that he was not the only person who had many probing questions to ask him.

Yet the court refused to let him question Allen. This was not an inquiry concerning Allen, his behaviour or, for that matter, the reasons why the man did what he did. He was not the main person under suspicion, Fennelly told Lee. The members of the court were not at all interested in Lee's questions. It was evident to them that Lee distrusted Allen hugely and they had no reason to concur. Still trying to make a point, Lee let the court know that Allen had assured him in France that, no matter how serious the accusations brought to Australia House were, Lee would never get his day in court. Lee wanted to know why the major had been so sure: who did he know in London and who were his friends?

He was not alone in distrusting Allen. When it was Quentin Spedding's turn to testify before the court, he made no secret of the fact that he disliked and distrusted the man. Spedding's superior at Australia House, General Hobbs, had liked Allen a great deal, and admired Allen for accepting his position for just two hundred pounds a year. Spedding asked the court what ulterior motive Allen could have had for accepting such a poorly paid position. Fennelly overruled this question, saying the court had no interest in Allen's ulterior motives. Spedding was sure that if the position the AIF offered had been a business proposition, Allen would never have accepted it. Fennelly simply told him again that the court had no interest at all in Allen's motives or finances.

To emphasise Allen's belittling nature, Spedding recounted an especially painful and embarrassing moment when he had stayed at the Hotel du Rhin at Amiens together with Allen. A friend of Allen's introduced them to a member of the South African war memorial section; this was a man Spedding had been particularly keen to meet because he had wanted to know if there would be any chance of finding a job in the war memorial department in South Africa. Allen's friend introduced Allen as 'Major Allen, Commanding Officer of the Australian Graves Services'.[11] And all the while Spedding, who was actually the OC, was standing next to them. Ignoring him completely, the other three carried on an animated discussion and in the end he had wandered away feeling insulted and belittled.

Spedding let the panel know that at Australia House letters had started coming to the office addressed to Allen as the 'Australian Officer in charge of the Graves Services'.[12] He appeared to have arranged some matters with the Red Cross as if he was the OC. Spedding had subsequently taken action, letting everyone know that it was actually he who was in command. He was not going to allow the man the run of the AGS if he could help it, he told the court. It had at the time been a matter of principle.

Spedding also had an axe to grind with Major Phillips, who reported that he had found the administration at Australia House more or less in a shambles after Spedding left in January. Spedding asked the court why they had not bothered to ask Colonel Hogben or any number of other people working at the AGS at the time about his administrative ability. It turned out that Major Phillips had opposed such a move and had strongly objected to others, especially those who had worked with Spedding, being called upon to give evidence.[13] He did not give any reason for this, but the court obviously did not find the request in any way out of the ordinary and went along with it. Spedding let the court know that he found it strange that Phillips had so much influence in regard to the proceedings that he had even managed to have Spedding's request to have one of his superiors vouch for him swept away.

By the end of January 1920, before there was any question of an inquiry being held, the situation at Australia House had become very unsatisfactory for Spedding. He told the court he had already been contemplating leaving the AGS when he was accused of a small matter of maladministration concerning a 'Duke'. He had voluntarily resigned his post. He wanted to go back to Australia and back to journalism; also, the high commissioner had suggested to him that his abilities might be needed elsewhere. When he was cleaning out his desk at Australia House one of the clerks came to him and told him that he had talked to Alfred Allen. The major had come in recently and let them know that Spedding would be leaving the office. Alfred Allen had suggested that he might well become the new OC in London in Spedding's place.[14]

Chapter 11
RE-ESTABLISHING THE AGS

The behaviour of the Australian men in the AGS had not gone unnoticed. Historian Charles Bean wrote in his diary that these Australians were by far 'the roughest lot of officers found in the AIF'.[1] William McBeath, who worked for the AGS, wrote home that although they had only been doing the work of reburying bodies for two weeks they already had two strikes with the men refusing to work until there were better means of handling the bodies, better food and all ceremonial parades had been cut.[2] Charlie Kingston, when first posted to Villers-Bretonneux, described his own men as a 'bad lot, inefficient, neither dependable nor reliable'.[3] Even Fabian Ware thought it would be a good idea to withdraw the Australians as soon as possible because 'they were getting up to much mischief'.[4]

The Australian Graves Services had been instituted to honour the memory of the AIF soldiers who had sacrificed their lives during the Great War. The men, left without much supervision, had created their own playground, bending the rules in such a way that they themselves lost any notion that their behaviour was unacceptable. Of course, not all men serving with the AGS were prone to improper behaviour—on the contrary, most of the men had volunteered out of sheer honest compassion for the fallen men and their families and had behaved accordingly.

The court concluded that the rotten apples would have to go. All of them. That meant removing Kingston, who was deemed unqualified and unfit for the job. Lieutenant Lee, who was found guilty of conduct unbecoming the character of an officer and gentleman. Bollen, who stood accused of nothing other than being a discontented grumbler but was highly disliked by most of the men, Coughlan and Billy Edwards for running estaminets and pimping, plus a number of others who had testified and made complaints. Then of course there was MacKay, who was accused of embezzling goods and also of stealing a car, and Wally Furby, who was his accomplice.

The court made a list of sixteen men who were to be discharged. In the end, none of them were prosecuted. Embedded in the rules of the court of inquiry was stated that the findings could never become part of the record of any man, could not constitute a charge and could not be offered in evidence.[5] Although the court had carefully considered the matter of retaining Kingston and Lee to be court-martialled, in the end it was decided that no good purpose would be served by implementing a form of punishment. The resultant harm of such a disclosure would far outweigh any good that could have been done,[6] although the members were not unanimous when it came to MacKay. Meikle found his fraudulent practices highly offensive but charging a soldier for misbehaviour would have no doubt drawn attention to what had happened, and under the circumstances that would have been highly undesirable. Sending the men back to Australia was justified as part of the ongoing demobilisation and as such would not attract any attention.

Most of the men had no idea that a court of inquiry was a confidential communication and thought they had gotten off lightly. They kept their mouths shut after returning to Australia, believing they could have easily ended up in gaol for the things they had done.

However merited the decision may have been, being kicked out of the army and sent home left a few men feeling extremely slighted. Lee, Kingston and Bollen did not understand how it was possible that neither Phillips nor Allen had been dismissed. The court had not even given them a rap on the knuckles, even though the witnesses believed both officers' leadership left much to be desired.

Phillips and Allen stayed and, with the 'rotten apples' gone, they were left in full control of the AGS. A few begrudging men, sent off to Australia just days after the inquiry, swore revenge. William Lee thought the whole inquiry had been a charade, devised to get rid of them all so they could be replaced by military police. Lee had left London in a furious state of mind and on the long boat trip back to the homeland he had plenty of time to plan a course of action.

The AGS went back to functioning as it previously had, albeit with some recommendations made to improve and revise aspects of the organisation.[7] The two court members, Fennelly and Meikle, as well as General Hobbs and High Commissioner Fisher made a number of recommendations to improve the structure and the organisation including that in France the situation would remain more or less the same with three representative officers in charge of different departments, with one senior officer in full charge of the entire organisation. AIF personnel, especially those on the photographic units, would be reduced as soon as possible and, where necessary, be replaced by civilians. New AGS personnel would be selected for their qualifications and/or previous good work. Suitable records would in future be kept of all spare parts, tyres and petrol.

As far as supervision of the men was concerned, one officer would be in charge of handling all disciplinary cases. Meikle and Fennelly also recommended that the camp at Villers-Bretonneux be abandoned and that headquarters be established at Arras. An office with an officer in charge at Poperinghe in the north as well as one in Amiens in the east would be enough to control the whole area.

It was General Hobbs who was strongly opposed to abandoning Villers-Bretonneux.[8] During the war, the small town had been a vital and strongly defended battleground for the Australians. Many lives had been lost in the area. In recognition of the Australian sacrifices, a memorial of thanks from the people of the town had been erected; Hobbs thought that turning their backs on the town at this stage would appear ungrateful. On top of that, one of the five Australian memorials to be erected in France would be placed in Villers-Bretonneux. The town was also situated very centrally, the roads making it easy to find and very accessible to anyone who wished to visit. In the end Hobbs got his way and it was decided that Villers-Bretonneux could stay. The new OC there would be William Meikle.

After the inquiry it became necessary to review the administrative organisation of the AGS in view of its long-term requirements. Thus, in May 1920, the Australian Graves Services received clear and explicit directions with regard to the tasks of its different units. Some recommendations to achieve this had been put down on paper by Colonel Hogben.[9] Six officers and 88 other ranks, approved by the AIF, were to continue to serve with the Australian Graves Services and it was expected that their assistance would be required for a further eighteen months, after which their appointment would be terminated.

The men would continue to work closely with the British exhumation parties, as well as locating the isolated AIF graves in conjunction with the British Army authorities. The goal was to find and reduce the numbers of soldiers reported as 'missing'. The men were also required to search the battle areas for graves that had not been found by the British exhumation parties. The areas were to be swept and re-swept, making sure no grave had been overlooked because once the area was given clearance any graves that had not been found would be regarded as lost. The men were to prepare and erect memorial crosses to the dead, compile and complete all burial records of Australians, photograph Australian graves and memorial crosses, and inspect cemetery areas where Australian soldiers were buried.

If relatives and friends wished to visit the graves, the men of the AGS were to act as guides and be willing to direct and guide any visitors searching for a specific grave. Australia House in London would be in charge of the records section, registry, photographic section, memorials and visits. The OC would be based at Australia House but would be required to make regular trips to France and Belgium in order to inspect and monitor the situation there.

By 1920, more than 30,000 Australian exhumation and reburial reports had been dealt with and about 16,000 men were still reported as missing. The minister for defence, Senator George Pearce, wanted the number of missing men to be reduced drastically. He found it an intolerable statistic and an embarrassment for the AIF.

The organisation in France was now to be extended from three to four locations. Its headquarters were to be at Villers-Bretonneux, with a senior inspector's group at Poperinghe, an assistant inspector's group at Amiens and a monumental section at Maricourt, about 31 miles south-east of Amiens. The senior inspector at Villers-Bretonneux, Captain Meikle, would be in charge of the administration, discipline and control of all the French areas and would report directly to Australia House.

Acquiring land proved a difficult task. Appointed by General Hobbs, Captain Barden negotiated the purchase of land for the memorial sites. The French were willing enough but sometimes more than thirteen different owners had to be dealt with to secure an area needed to create a decent cemetery. Then title deeds had to be registered in Paris. In Pozières the townspeople

Major General Sir Fabian Arthur Goulstone Ware was the founder of the Imperial War Graves Commission, now the Commonwealth War Graves Commission.

Lieutenant Robert David Burns, standing on the right.

Andrew Fisher served as
Australia's second High
Commissioner to the United
Kingdom from 1 January
1916 until 1 January 1921.

Australia House, The Strand, London.

Although the enemy, the Red Baron was held in high esteem by the allies. His burial attracted many mourners.

After the war somewhere between Amiens and Villers-Bretonneux.
(Ivan Bawtree photo courtesy of J. Gordon-Smith)

A British grave
recovery unit at
work. (Ivan Bawtree
photo courtesy of
J. Gordon-Smith)

A grave site near the Belgian border. (Photo Ivan Bawtree courtesy of J. Gordon-Smith)

Unidentified members of the Australian War Graves Detachment at work at Villers-Bretonneux cemetery.

The self-declared 'Major' Alfred Allen, otherwise known as Captain Allen.

Lieutenant General J.J. Talbot Hobbs, who was very impressed with Alfred Allen.

Soldiers marching through Poperinghe around 1917.

An officer with two women in front of an Estaminet. (Ivan Bawtree photo courtesy of J. Gordon-Smith)

The inside of an Estaminet. (Ivan Bawtree photo courtesy of J. Gordon-Smith)

Ettie Rout (middle) with Australians at Villers-Bretonneux in 1919.

Ettie Rout with unidentified Australian soldiers.

Unveiling the boys' school at Villers-Bretonneux. Australian children from Victoria helped fund the school.

The Red Chateau before the war. The proprietor at the time was Madam Henriette Delacour. After the war the chateau became the home of the Australian Graves Detachment.

Five officers of the Australian Graves Detachment gathered in front of their offices on the grounds of the Red Chateau.

The Motor Transport Section of the Australian Graves Detachment at Villers-Bretonneux in June 1919.

The Nissen huts on the grounds of the Red Chateau where Australian Graves Detachment personnel lived.

A Frank Hurley composite photograph.

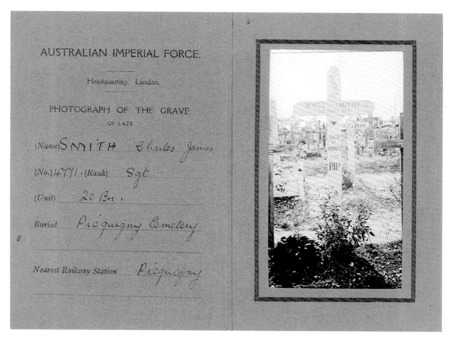

An example of the photograph and particulars bereaved families at home received
from the AIF.

Senator George Foster Pearce demanded an inquiry be undertaken into the Australian Graves Service.

Alfred Allen and his daughter. (Photo courtesy of Jenny van Middeldijk)

Stonemasons making the headstones that would replace the wooden crosses on the graves. (Ivan Bawtree photo courtesy of J. Gordon-Smith)

Poppies planted by Rose Venn-Brown growing on graves in France.

Finding the remains of a soldier in the mud of Flanders. (Ivan Bawtree photo courtesy of J. Gordon-Smith)

Philip Fennelly presided over the first Court of Inquiry.

William Thomas Meikle was accused by William Lee of being bribed as a member of the Court of Inquiry.

General William Birdwood. (Courtesy of the State Library of Victoria)

Colonel James Burns, Robert Burns' father.

Mary Elizabeth Chomley

Vera Deakin set up an Australian graves registration unit first in Egypt and later in London.

Elizabeth Chomley worked with the Red Cross and was especially involved with Australian prisoners of war.

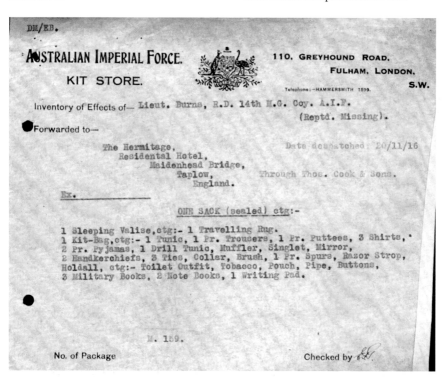

DM/EB.

AUSTRALIAN IMPERIAL FORCE.

KIT STORE.

110, GREYHOUND ROAD,
FULHAM, LONDON,
S.W.

Telephone:—HAMMERSMITH 1899.

Inventory of Effects of— Lieut. Burns, R.D. 14th M.G. Coy. A.I.F.
(Reptd. Missing).

Forwarded to—

The Hermitage,
Residental Hotel,
Maidenhead Bridge,
Taplow,
England.

Date despatched: 20/11/16

Through Thos. Cook & Sons.

Ex.

ONE SACK (sealed) ctg:-

1 Sleeping Valise,ctg:- 1 Travelling Rug.
1 Kit-Bag,ctg:- 1 Tunic, 1 Pr. Trousers, 1 Pr. Puttees, 3 Shirts,
2 Pr. Pyjamas, 1 Drill Tunic, Muffler, Singlet, Mirror,
2 Handkerchiefs, 3 Ties, Collar, Brush, 1 Pr. Spurs, Razor Strop,
Holdall, ctg:- Toilet Outfit, Tobacco, Pouch, Pipe, Buttons,
3 Military Books, 2 Note Books, 1 Writing Pad.

M. 159.

No. of Package

Checked by

The inventory of Robert Burns' belongings sent to his father.

British colonel, Alfred Sutton, with an
unknown chid in 1919.

Australian grave diggers in France.

Lieutenant Robert David Burns' headstone erected
in 2010, ninety-four years after his death.

and the mayor opposed the purchase of a six-acre block, and in other instances plots were not bought because the owners asked unreasonable prices. When a site was purchased, it had to be cleared of rubble before it was fenced and gravel pathways were laid, then concrete shelters and posts and chains had to be erected.

The military advisor at Australia House, Lieutenant Colonel Percy Buckley, managed to persuade the Australian government to keep funding the AGS in spite of all the difficulties. Buckley, a former member of the Royal Australian Engineers, was appointed staff officer for military administration of the AIF in the office of the Australian high commissioner in 1915. He assured the government that 'the work that is being done is in every way justified and that the results achieved are very satisfactory'. He did acknowledge, however, that the work was 'most disagreeable in all its aspects' and that it was not an easy matter to keep the men happy. Men were continually sent home for going off the rails, although they were often praised by Buckley for having 'performed their task well'.[10]

It was of the utmost essence that the existing gravesites and the men serving in the AGS were well organised and well supervised. Now that the war was over, many families were looking for ways to visit the former battlefields. Some wanted to personally pay their respects at the established graves of their sons, husbands and fathers; others, less fortunate, had only a letter or a cable message to indicate that their family member was 'missing', and they felt the need to go in search of a loved one's remains.

By May 1920, it was possible for Australians wanting to visit gravesites in Belgium and France to do so through a scheme created by the British YMCA. The YMCA had built hostels near the various cemeteries to meet all requirements at a low cost. Everyone was convinced that visitors would come. Already scattered groups of Australians had been spotted wandering across the countryside asking for directions to cemeteries.

When Major Phillips was appointed AGS head of staff at Australia House, managing the AGS from London with Allen and Meikle tending to matters in France, all appeared to be slowly settling down.

But Lee, who was determined to rock the boat, did just that when he returned to Australia.

Chapter 12
ROCKING THE BOAT

Billy Lee was not the only one who had returned to Australia determined to have his say. The first articles in Australia's newspapers about the dysfunctional Australian Graves Services appeared in November 1920 when Will Bollen's wife, Janet, wrote to the editor of the Melbourne *Age* about the disgusting state of the gravesites in France. 'I would advise relatives to wait before going on their sad pilgrimage,' she wrote. 'I feel confident that the work is being positively neglected.'[1]

Once he was back home, Lee forwarded his complaints to the prime minister and the minister for defence, Senator Pearce. They were elaborate, somewhat rambling fifteen-page letters in which he begged for another hearing, this time in Australia. He accused Phillips and Allen of bribing Fennelly and Meikle, promising them plum AGS jobs if they ruled that Lee and Kingston should be sent home. He felt he had not been properly heard in France as the inquiry had not originated from his own complaints but had been the result of Willoughby Bollen's.

Lee was clearly determined to do everything in his power to get a new inquiry underway, far from the biased AIF in London. In his letters he threatened to take the matter to parliament, to the press, or even to the House of Representatives if need be.[2] It became evident that Lee would keep on demanding until he was given his day in court.

He believed his dismissal had been unjust, and he blamed Allen and Phillips for it. In court Allen had described Lee's attitude as openly hostile; Major Allen was about to find out how openly hostile Lee could be. Lee would let the world know about the wire-pulling and scheming performed by Major Phillips in that 'mock' court, all of it supported by the conniving Alfred Allen. During the inquiry, Allen had boasted that he could do the whole of the work in France and Belgium alone. Lee felt it was ludicrous; it was a statement made by a malicious man with no other objective than to make Lee appear inadequate and incompetent. Lee was determined to take the man down.

Accompanying his letter to Senator Pearce, in which he requested an inquiry, Lee sent a sheet with an extensive list of questions he wanted to lay before Alfred Allen.[3] There was also a long list of witnesses Lee wished to be heard, living in both Australia and Europe.

Within days he received a 'no' from the secretary of the defence department. The matter had received careful consideration both in France and England and Lee's letter had produced no new grounds to reopen the case or start a new one. The decision by responsible authorities overseas would not be disturbed and would stand as it was. There was a financial reason to discourage a reopening of the case—the authorities in France as well as in Australia felt that such an inquiry, held on two different continents, would not only become problematic but also far too expensive.

However, just weeks later other disturbing articles about the Australian Graves Services in France began finding their way into the Australian tabloids. William Babington Dynes sent a letter to the press expressing his concern about the condition of the cemeteries in France.[4] Dynes had served with the AIF until October 1919 and had just recently returned to Europe to visit the graves of a few friends and family members. The article was very graphic about the state of the Australian war graves.

In it, Dynes explained to the public that they should expect very little in regard to the construction and condition of the sites for quite some time. Dynes wrote that the huge military machine that had been established in early 1919 to carry out the Imperial War Graves Commission's ideas seemed like a flywheel that had failed to gyrate. He described the AGS as 'an organisation consisting of spare parts, in which inefficiency, bungle and waste were the leading rods'.[5]

To Dynes the results of the past year could be categorised as nil. The Australian Graves Services had become a hopeless wreck, due to lack of management. Dynes had returned to France expecting to find at least a few presentable gravesites, but he found the places he visited unkempt and bleak. Three months prior to his visit, a group of men with horticultural backgrounds had been plucked from the AIF to beautify the spots where their comrades lay, but nothing had been planted nor any grass laid that he could see when he was there. The poppies that Rose Venn-Brown had once planted had died and the cemeteries were now bleak spots in the countryside—shoddy, muddy and in disarray. Dynes was fully conscious of the implications of what he was saying, but he 'could not be an onlooker at the present state of affairs knowing that many might well travel thousands of miles. The matter demanded urgent attention'.

Concern mounted as articles and letters were published. Letters from anxious relatives found their way to Australia House. Undesirable public controversy was starting to develop and the minister for defence, Senator Pearce, demanded an update on matters in France. There were hurried exchanges between Pearce and both the AIF and Australia House about Lee and the letters Pearce had received.

Major Phillips sent Pearce a telegram. As tactfully as he could, he suggested that the problem had been sufficiently dealt with by the court in France. Not one court martial had been referred to a military court, and all hearings had been held in secret and closed to the public.

Now that a wave of public controversy was emerging, Pearce realised that heated feelings might get totally out of control if nothing was done. It was General Birdwood who somewhat unexpectedly came to the rescue.

General William Riddell Birdwood, a British army officer, had served on the staff of Lord Kitchener during the Second Boer War and had gone on to become commander of the Australian and New Zealand Army Corps during the Gallipoli campaign in 1915.[6] He was commander-in-chief of the Fifth Army on the Western Front during the closing stages of the war. Although always highly popular among his men, public admiration for the general peaked when he visited Australia and New Zealand in the early months of 1920. For the Australians, he was the 'Soul of Anzac', and wherever he made an appearance he drew large crowds who were eager to get a glimpse of the man.

As he travelled the country, Birdwood laid foundations to commemorate those who had died in the Great War. He went to dances and concerts and dined with local mayors, and he was renowned for his speeches in which he commemorated the diggers and their comrades, who had so generously headed to Europe to confront the foe, with many of them losing their lives as a result. Lauded and applauded by all who met him, he slowly developed into an icon.

Birdwood and Pearce had known each other from the beginning of the war. In May 1915 Birdwood temporarily took command of the AIF and, together with Pearce, they searched the AIF for competent officers to appoint to commands and staff.[7]

It had been a difficult process to find professionally trained officers; the Australians were known for their casual attitude towards the war. The British complained about Birdwood's relaxed disciplinary methods and about the Australian soldiers' behaviour, which totally conflicted with the British Army's traditions. In February 1918, British Field Marshal Douglas Haig wrote in a letter to his wife: 'We have had to separate the Australians into Convalescent Camps of their own, because they were giving so much trouble when along with our men and put such revolutionary ideas into their heads.'[8]

In May 1918 Birdwood finally handed over the corps to Lieutenant General John Monash and later set off on his tour of New Zealand and Australia. 'Birdie' was immensely popular among soldiers and civilians alike, so who better to reassure the public and put people's minds at ease? The people would undoubtedly listen to his opinion. So, after his celebrated trip around Australia, Birdwood left for France.

Birdwood was aware of the problems arising from the AGS and also aware of how damaging it could become. He would go to France and do his best to help turn things around.

Chapter 13
THE BODY DIVINER

What Birdwood did not know was that, prior to his visit to France, another scandal involving members of the AGS had cropped up. Alfred Allen and Major George Phillips were now the accused, and it involved a piece of subterfuge concerning the body of the son of a respected Australian colonel and businessman. The AIF had barely managed to douse the flames of its first humiliation before a second one was popping out of the bag.

A worrying development was that families were now beginning to focus on how to travel to Europe to pay respect to their loved ones. So far they had only trickled into the country in small numbers but, thanks to the British YMCA, accommodation and guides for those who did make the pilgrimage were in the process of being set up. Already, during the early months of 1920, commercial operators, out to make a profit, were advertising their accommodated tours to the battlefields in Australian newspapers.

People who booked these unauthorised trips to France and Belgium sometimes found themselves stranded and returned home with alarming stories. Most of the tour operators had no experience in this field. They expected cemeteries and accommodations to be prominently signposted, but once in France tour guides were often at a loss in the French countryside. Sometimes it was even the tour guide's first trip to France.

As they were escorted through the countryside, it became evident to the pilgrims that the hired guides had no idea where the cemeteries were located and often no accommodation had been arranged in advance. Information from the locals was difficult to come by and the Australian guides found themselves faced with French or Flemish people who did not speak a word of English.

When a cemetery was finally located, the visitors were often surprised and disappointed to find that they were not exclusively reserved for Australians. Sometimes a sign was put up by the British to indicate that Australians were interred there, but often there was nothing in place to signify where Australians were buried. These poorly organised pilgrimages in some cases ended in disaster, with pilgrims left stranded in France or Belgium by tour operators who had taken their money only to abandon them.[1]

For those not able to make the trip to Europe, arrangements to put a wreath on a loved one's grave were made by charity organisations. A basic wreath adorned with a simple message could be organised from Australia for a few shillings. Most of the organisations were honest and sincere, but shameful profiteering also occurred.[2]

When a relative ordered a floral tribute from one of the unscrupulous firms based in France or Belgium, the wreath would often not be delivered. Using fabricated photography, these shysters would inform mourners in Australia that their instructions had been carried out. Often the same photograph was sent to different people over and over again. Bad photography prevented a clear vision of the name on the headstone, and one headstone looked pretty much the same as the next in any case.

After these scams had been publicly exposed, Australian firms started up their own businesses providing floral tributes. Advertising 'a piece of home' to be sent overseas, wattle was refrigerated and loaded onto ships heading for Europe.[3]

As whole communities struggled to come to terms with the enormity of their loss, there was a call to assist with travelling costs. One of those pleas came from a bereaved mother, Jane MacMillan, who had lost her son Ronald at Zonnebeke.[4] She approached the prime minister. Because Australia's distance from Europe was so great, Mrs MacMillan asked the government for an assisted passage to the battlefields. However, with over 50,000 Australian war casualties, the government did not think their responsibility extended as far as funding assisted passages.

At the beginning of 1920, trustworthy tours were being set up with the help of well-known Australian shipping merchants and travel agencies. One of them was the English company Thomas Cook and its branch in Australia, Cooks Travel Agency in Melbourne; another was Burns Philp and Company, one of whose owners was James Burns, the father of Lieutenant Robert Burns, who had lost his life near Fromelles in the war.[5]

These trips were reasonably priced. From London the cost was five to seven pounds for a four-day tour. This included railway charges (third class in England, and second class in France and Belgium), full board and lodging, plus the services of capable representatives who would advise and accompany the travellers. What was not included was the cost of passports, nor any transport between England and Australia.[6]

It was only a matter of time before more people would begin to avail themselves of this opportunity, but Pearce did not want those who went to France to return to Australia with stories that could damage the Australian Graves Services. High Commissioner Fisher was quick to discourage mass trips to Europe; he knew that most pilgrims would suffer disappointment when they came to the battlefields and he expected it would be well into 1920 before the cemeteries would be presentable enough for any visitors.[7] People who knew their loved ones were yet to be found posed an extra problem as they randomly scoured the countryside in search of a grave or a body. By the end of June 1920 some 30 Australians a week were crossing over to England and France to visit graves.

In the months after the first inquiry, Colonel Hogben and Senator Pearce both concluded that it would help boost public opinion if the AGS in France could increase the number of men found and identified on the battlefields. Hogben didn't like all those crosses marked as 'unknown' soldiers one bit and in a newspaper interview he let the public know that he would do everything in his power to put a name to a cross.[8] A good example was Poperinghe in Belgium; there all 150 graves had a name.

An interesting proposal was then submitted to the Commonwealth government from one of the officers working in the graves unit in France.[9] Captain Meikle, the member of the court who had since taken up a position at the newly established headquarters at Villers-Bretonneux, stated that in practical terms the majority of the missing were identifiable, owing to the place and circumstances in which they were found.

The strict rule up to this point had been that the crosses over the graves should not bear any name unless identification was absolutely positive. Meikle was now suggesting that it would be better to chance an occasional mistake than to leave many thousands nameless. In other words, one finds a body, picks a name from the list of those missing in the same spot and attaches a random name to the body. Some thought this was indeed an 'interesting' proposal.

Even the Australian prime minister, Billy Hughes, suggested the creation of empty graves on which the names of those who were missing should be inscribed so that families could mourn their dead in a precise location.[10] However, Fabian Ware became concerned that the Imperial War Graves Commission's work might become subject to question if this became commonplace and insisted that the one thing that must be avoided was an impression of 'fake'. While others thought of the proposal as 'a happy solution to many difficulties', Rudyard Kipling, whose son had gone missing in France, let Ware know that he found the idea of a grave carrying an identification, without anyone being sure it contained the correct body, more than 'distasteful'. The empty grave would have constituted a lie that discredited the work of the IWGC, deceiving the families who had put their trust in it. For those involved, it became clear that if anything was to be done about the 'missing', it would have to be in a way that did not create the illusion of an actual grave.[11]

———■———

For the men who had been sent home after the first AGS inquiry, the suspicion arose that the proposal to 'fake' a grave could have been whispered to Meikle by Alfred Allen.

For months Allen had been finding bodies all over France and attaching names to them; he was becoming something of a hero in the process.[12] It aroused considerable suspicion that a man with no military background was finding bodies strewn around the countryside and in the process was able to identify them, whereas the British, with all their know-how and knowledge, had failed to match this singular achievement. Maybe the authorities were willing to look the other way. After all the negative news about the Australian Graves Services, the department could do with a hero. Major Alfred Allen fit the brief. He appeared to be one made of the right stuff, with an impeccable character to boot.

English writer John Oxenham was one of the first to describe Alfred Allen's remarkable ability to find missing men.[13] Oxenham wrote enthusiastically: 'When all hope of finding a body has been given up by everyone else, one can turn to Major Allen as a last resort. In eight out of ten cases Allen solves the mystery setting the seal of certainty on lingering hopes and doubts at home.' Oxenham described Allen as 'a "big" man, bodily, mentally and spiritually. A hearty good fellow, fiercely outspoken and unbindable by red tape'. Oxenham's advice was: 'If you cannot find any trace of a missing AIF man then ask Major Allen.'

Allen had explained to Oxenham his modus operandi. After receiving a request to locate a missing body from Major Phillips at Australia House, Allen would set out with his divining rod. Phillips would send Allen the coordinates of where the missing person was last sighted and to what battalion he had been attached. Allen then journeyed to the place, surveyed the ground and took bearings. Sometimes the ground had been previously checked for bodies many times over by burial parties and declared 'clean'. It was only when Allen probed the ground delicately with his trusty steel rod, in all the likely places, that the ground magically yielded its secrets to him. According to Oxenham, the major found 70 to 100 dead men a week, mostly on already-cleared areas.

Living with his men at Bird Cage Camp in Poperinghe, Allen's domicile was anything but luxurious. Poperinghe was a town where many roads intersected. It had been a mainly British garrison town during the war where soldiers, supplies, information and everything else going to the front lines passed through daily. With the constant influx of soldiers and refugees, the town's pre-war population of 11,000 had doubled during the hostilities. Now that the war had ended and with all the demobilisation going on, 'Pops' was becoming a quieter place, although most of the wartime breweries had remained as had quite a few women of ill repute.

Bird Cage Camp, where Allen resided, was situated at the edge of the town, on the road to Hazebrouk. A former

British camp, it comprised a collection of wooden huts and duckboards next to a big barbed wire cage where German prisoners had been held during the war. The Belgians used the word *vogelkooi* (birdcage) to describe the Allied pens where German POWs were held. Although the accommodation could easily be described as spartan, the British huts were often much better than the Australian ones. The English were known for their appreciation of homeliness, and some of the huts even had petite gardens and decorated walls.

Nonetheless, Lee, Gray and Furby—some of the men who had been sent home—had always found it strange that a convinced Quaker like Allen would feel at home so close to a town that allowed alcohol and sex to flow very freely. There appeared to be no need for the major to stay there for financial reasons.

As a successful Sydney architect before the war, Alfred Allen had owned an island on the harbour. Engineering had been his hobby and he owned offices in Australia and South Africa. He was said to have constructed a water-cooled motor that had been patented in London. Spedding was also one of the men who questioned the major's motives to live in such a place, busying himself with such a gruesome job. There was no financial reason to do so and Spedding could hardly believe that Allen acted out of honourable motives.[14]

Contrary to Oxenham's words, most of the AGS men knew there was nothing magical about the exhumations of bodies. To pull up sacks of green slime from the earth, you needed either a strong stomach or strong belief. Was it the major's faith that was driving him on? Or was it something else?

On 12 March 1919, Quentin Spedding received a letter asking about the whereabouts of the grave of a Lieutenant Robert Burns. He was in the middle of organising the new Australian Graves Services and left the letter lying in a drawer for a while. In September 1919 a request came from Sam MacMillan asking Allen to assist in finding the body. According to the letter, the Germans had stated that there were five large mass graves at Fromelles before Pheasant Wood. Burns's body was most likely interred in one of these graves.[15] MacMillan asked Allen to search the area. At that time Allen had been dealing with the conflict between Lee and Kingston, and he also left this request sitting in a drawer for months.

It was Major Phillips who received another request from the Red Cross asking if anything had been done about the matter. The father of the man who had gone missing was a former colonel and an important businessman, and another family member had been sending letters asking about the body. Allen replied on 22 January that he had not been able to search the area but hoped to sometime during the next week.[16] When another letter reached him, Allen quickly realised the urgency of the request. He became very prompt in finding Robert Burns's grave.

He let Australia House know that he had found a cross placed by the Germans at Fournes-en-Weppes about two miles down the road from Fromelles and had decided, on the spur of the moment, that this was where the lieutenant must lie. Although the Red Cross had clearly noted that the Germans had given the location of the body as being buried at Fromelles, Allen concluded that the grave at Fournes must be the one implied. Allen informed Burns's relatives that he had encountered great difficulties in finding the spot and had scoured the countryside for a week looking for Robert Burns's body.[17] Walking around Fromelles, Pheasant Wood and a portion of Fournes, he was able to locate what he thought must be the accurate gravesite. He appeared very proud of his find.

It was only when a family member demanded to be present at the exhumation to personally identify the body that the major began to show doubts about the location and about the possibility of it actually containing the body of Robert Burns.

Chapter 14
THE COLONEL'S SON

There is a dreadful finality about the act of sending back to the bereaved the sad reminders of their loved ones. Colonel James Burns received his youngest son's death voucher months after he had gone missing. All it said was that Robert had fallen in the neighbourhood of Fromelles around 20 July 1916. But as a parent you don't really lose hope. If there is no certainty then there is always hope.

A statement by the CO, J.W. Kershaw of the 5th Machine Gun, reached James Burns. Kershaw said that Robert Burns 'was last seen after the German counter-attack had succeeded on both flanks and it is supposed that he was killed whilst visiting the left flank of the 14th Brigade'.[1] The identification disc among his belongings came from Germany. No particulars were presented except that the officer was deceased. Burns was reported as killed in action by the Anzac Section of the War Office in a letter dated 24 February 1917. A note on file in

German read: '*Lieut. Burns, R.D. 14.M.G.K. (Australier) am 19.7. im Gegend Fromelles gefallen*'[2] (Lieutenant Burns, RD, 14 M.G.K. [Australian] died on 19.7. in the Fromelles region). But a conflicting report had come to James Burns saying that Robert had been taken to a German hospital with severe wounds.

When the Red Cross finally sent Robert's belongings to him in November 1916, James Burns was staying at the Hermitage Hotel at Taplow, England. As he touched his son's possessions—his sleeping valise, his travelling rug, tunic, trousers, shirts, pyjamas, handkerchiefs, ties, tobacco, pipe and notebooks—they brought home to him the possibility and reality of Robert's death. But the fact that these items had not actually been plucked from his body left a glimmer of hope.

The colonel knew he would have to wait until the end of the war to find out what exactly had happened to his son. Until that time, he would treat the boy's life as ended, but with a small reserve of doubt.

James Burns had come to Australia from Scotland in 1862, when he was only sixteen. He had settled in Queensland and opened a shop at Townsville; soon afterwards he started a shipping service between Sydney and Townsville. He went on to become the managing director of the shipping firm Burns Philp and Company of Bridge Street, Sydney.

Away from his business life, Burns became associated with the volunteer movement. In 1891, he was appointed captain of the Parramatta Mounted Troops and in 1897 he took command of the New South Wales Lancer Regiment with the rank of colonel. In 1908 Burns retired from the military forces after having commanded the Australian 1st Light Horse Brigade. He had married, Mary Susan Lemington, in 1875, but she had passed away in 1904, leaving him three sons and three daughters.[3]

James Burns was a stern, somewhat unapproachable father for his daughters and sons; he led his family much as he managed his businesses. After the war broke out, his sons saw active duty in France, something their father took for granted and deemed nothing more than their duty to God and country. But when his youngest son died it hit a nerve, and it became difficult for this strict and aloof man to come to terms with the boy's death. In a last letter, Robert had let his family know that the preparations for battle were gruelling. The flies and heat had been a pest in Egypt, but in France the great demotivating factor was the seemingly constant rainfall.

It was hard not knowing how and when his son had died. Like most bereaved, James Burns could not stop himself from imagining what had happened to Robert. Visions of his son dying suddenly and instantly alternated in his thoughts with visions of Robert suffering a slow harsh death on the battlefield. But Robert might even have ended up in a German hospital. Always the most optimistic and comforting thought for any bereaved is that a missing family member might be still alive.

James and his children hoped to be able to lay it all to rest once they had found Robert's body and had buried their brother and son, giving him a decent grave. While the war had been going on it had been impossible to roam the countryside looking for a body. James's only peculiar comfort was that Robert had not been the only one in his division to die that day. There were 173 Australian soldiers from the 5th Division AIF listed among the missing at Fromelles and he had been told that more than 5000 Australians had lost their lives during the battle of Fromelles from 19 to 20 July 1916.

In those first years after the death of Robert Burns, the news from Europe was remorseless and grim. As the Germans marauded their way across Belgium, James Burns promised himself that once the war had ended he would do everything in his power to find Robert.

On 10 January 1919, a few months after the end of hostilities, Burns sent a letter to the Red Cross requesting any information they might have about his son.[4] He wanted to know if Robert had been buried singly or in a common grave along with others, or if he was perhaps captured and still being held in an enemy prison camp. To find out whether his son might be interred in a German POW camp or whether he was undeniably deceased, Burns turned to the Australian Red Cross in London run by Miss Vera Deakin. Deakin had been one of the first people to set up a Wounded and Missing service.

—■—

When the first lists of the Australian casualties at Gallipoli were published, as far as most people were aware, news about the fate of their soldier relatives could only be obtained through the Australian Imperial Force Base Records Office, located in Melbourne. But dealing with the Base Records Office was a frustrating process for most families. The office, soon overwhelmed by correspondence from families and having no experience with such an enormous number of requests, was painfully slow to obtain information from overseas. Its staff was more often than not just as badly informed as the bereaved families and could often do very little for them.

When Vera Deakin, youngest daughter of Alfred Deakin, arrived in Cairo in 1914, she was quick to understand the need for an organisation that could inform the families if a soldier had died, was wounded or had gone missing.[5] She quickly went to work to set up an Australian Wounded and Missing Inquiry Bureau. When the Australians moved to the Western Front in 1916, the bureau shifted its headquarters to London. In London, Deakin, together with Elizabeth Maud Chomley, an Australian living in London, scoured the official lists of the wounded and missing soldiers as well as interviewing soldiers in the English hospitals and camps. Chomley was secretary of the prisoners of war branch of the Australian Red Cross, London and Deakin was head of the Wounded and Missing Department.

Chomley was a rather daunting woman, very strong-willed and determined.[6] She worked tirelessly to find out as much information as she could and remove all doubt about the fate of individual soldiers. To cope with the mass of requests coming from the bereaved at home asking for help investigating the whereabouts of sons and husbands, the two women mobilised a large body of volunteers. Particularly concerned with prisoners of war, they aimed to trace missing soldiers and to provide information to their families. They also sent thousands of parcels to Australians in German camps, making sure the internees knew they had not been forgotten.

The conditions the Australian POWs endured varied greatly. In 1917 many were held in appalling conditions at Fort MacDonald near Lille on the French–Belgian border. Some starved and were treated brutally, working for months under shellfire close behind German lines. As in all camps, whether Allied or German, questions of hygiene posed a problem. Built in haste, the goal was to erect a maximum number of installations, and that relegated sanitary considerations to the backburner.

Camps in Germany featured only a simple tap in the yard that had to service thousands of people. Very often latrines consisted of a simple board with a hole in the middle above a pit, which the prisoners were tasked with emptying at regular intervals. Because of their very basic construction, the toilets often overflowed during powerful rains, creating an unbreathable atmosphere in the camps. Diseases such as typhus or cholera appeared very quickly.

Despite this, conditions in the German camps were better than those in Belgium and France, but prisoners suffered increasingly from food shortages caused by the British blockade. From the start of their captivity, food posed a problem for prisoners. They complained of a diet that was too inconsistent to ward off the hunger pangs they felt. Many survived only because of Chomley's regular Red Cross parcels. Chomley also sent two lots of clothing a year to the camps, most of which came from English factories. There were restrictions, but the German authorities often allowed parcels to go through for the Australians. 'They used to think that the Australians were ferocious people, and would rise up if not treated well,' she once said. 'I used to encourage that feeling.'[7]

In their searches for men, whether missing or prisoners of war, Deakin and Chomley found their work by no means easy; their dealings with the army were often testing. The military regularly confronted them with suspicion and even jealousy. Their branches of the Red Cross became the only alternative source the relatives had and they were frequently regarded as a court of appeal for those who were unsuccessful in obtaining information from the military authorities. They found themselves dealing with hundreds of letters every week.

—■—

Still hoping for any sign of his son being alive, James Burns received a letter from the Red Cross just a few weeks after his January letter of inquiry; it informed him that, although his son's name had appeared on a German list of the dead, the Red Cross had never succeeded in obtaining any other information about him, except that he had fallen in the region of Fromelles. However, they had added his name to a list of missing men they circulated among the returned prisoners and in all the camps and hospitals in England.

In February Burns suggested that the Red Cross might now be able to communicate directly with the German authorities and that they may be able to give him a more complete report on what actually happened to his son. Robert's identity disc had come back from the Germans some time ago—could they check if the boy had been taken from the battlefield wounded? He might have died in a German hospital. Making it clear that he was prepared to meet any expense that was considered necessary in order to find out what had happened to his son and ultimately to recover his body, he waited for a reply.

It came just a few days later. The Red Cross let him know that there was no burial report for his son, official or unofficial. The first request from James Burns had gone to the AIF graves detachment but the Red Cross promised to hand the request over to the Australian Graves Services shortly, which was in the process of being set up. Burns wrote back asking when he could expect the Australian Graves Services to answer his questions and requesting the name of the secretary of the AGS, as well as the address of their office.[8]

Spedding's contact details were sent to Burns by the Australian Red Cross. The Red Cross also sent Burns a letter from the German authorities now confirming that Lieutenant Robert Burns had been buried in a mass grave in the neighbourhood of Fromelles in France.

With the knowledge that his son had very likely been killed and buried by the Germans, James Burns, together with his children, became highly motivated to locate the grave. Burns wrote to the AGS asking if it had any information on the exact whereabouts of his son's grave. After receiving this letter, Spedding gave it to one of his staff who sent it on to Allen, who stuffed it in a drawer and forgot about it in the chaos of those first months of setting up the AGS.

James Burns waited patiently. But after some months, not wishing to stay in London any longer, he decided to appoint a representative from the Burns Philp and Company London office to pursue the investigation further. The old man's health was deteriorating and he wanted to return to Australia; the cold and damp weather in London was adding to his distress. The man Burns appointed to relentlessly probe the AGS in a quest to find the location of his son's body was Cecil Arkell Smith.

Chapter 15
TAKING ACTION

Cecil Smith, appointed by James Burns to find out where Robert's body had been buried, was both an official of the Bank of New South Wales and the London representative of Burns's shipping company during the search; his wife was James Burns's niece.

James Burns was already in his seventies and his health had begun to fluctuate. He was also still a very busy man. As co-owner of an extensive shipping company, he found himself too old and frail to go trudging around the French countryside in an effort to locate his son's grave. His eldest son, James, had come back from the war and was needed in the business. His middle son had come back an invalid with persistent health problems. His three daughters were just as keen to find Robert as he was but they did not have any desire to scour the country, so he chose the husband of his niece who had been a childhood friend of Robert. Smith was a determined man and Burns was sure he would do everything in his power to find his wife's cousin's body.

Although James Burns had started writing to the Red Cross seeking information about his son's whereabouts at the beginning of 1919, he had been told to wait until the Australian Graves Services had been properly set up, and so he backed off for some months. The Red Cross had sent a letter in March 1919 to Horseferry Road inquiring whether the AIF could look into the matter, but nothing happened.[1] It appeared to Smith that everyone had forgotten about it. Alfred Allen, who had been assigned to the job, had not taken the trouble to get back to him at all.

More than a year later, Smith decided to pay a visit to Australia House to ask in person what had happened to the request sent to them so long ago. At Australia House Lieutenant Sam MacMillan, officer in charge of the Graves Registration Branch of the AIF, met him.[2]

MacMillan had been a journalist in Sydney before the war. Although Smith and he had never met previously, MacMillan knew the Burns case as he had written to Alfred Allen just a few months previously to ask him if any progress had been made in regard to the search for Burns. But the case did not appear to be on Allen's priority list and his letter had not even been answered. Now unexpectedly being confronted by Smith, MacMillan was caught by surprise. However, he was aware of whom he was dealing with and more than willing to oblige the man who now faced him.

The records showed that on 12 March 1919 a letter from the Red Cross, addressed to the corps burial officer of the Australian Graves Services at Australia House in London, had arrived.[3] The letter to 'The Body Snatcher', as the burial officer was known to the men in the AIF, asked for the place of burial of Lieutenant Robert Burns, whose body was very likely to be found near Fromelles.[4] The records also contained a communication from Germany that stated that there were five large mass graves at Pheasant Wood, on the outskirts of Fromelles, and another (No.1.M.43) in a German military cemetery at Fournes-en-Weppes. MacMillan had sent a digest of these facts on to the senior officer at Poperinghe, Alfred Allen, requesting a search be made.

At the end of 1919 James Burns sent another request to the Red Cross and then, on 16 January 1920, after hearing nothing at all from Allen, another communication was sent urgently requesting an answer and asking for a result. Allen reacted to this second communication on 24 January, simply letting the acting secretary for the high commissioner know that it had not been possible to arrange a search up to this time. He did not explain why it had not been possible, only that he had not got around to it.

When another communication arrived from Spedding, informing him that Robert Burns's family would be visiting Australia House asking for news, Allen finally put in some effort. Realising who he was dealing with and sensing the urgency in the communications, Allen sent word back only a few days later that he had now been to Fournes and had discovered a mass British grave there, with a cross bearing a German inscription that stated that English soldiers had been buried there.

In the meantime, Major George Phillips had taken over command from Quentin Spedding and he had just come to office when another letter from Allen arrived. The letter stated that Allen believed that the cross he had found earlier at Fournes was actually the cross that marked Robert Burns's grave.[5] Warrant Officer Peter Wilkie forwarded the letter to Smith. In the letter Allen did not explain how and why he had come to this conclusion, but for the Burns family this did not matter.

Smith was over the moon, believing he could finally tell his uncle that Robert's grave had been located. Smith had no reason to regard the find other than genuine. He sent word to Robert's sisters, two of whom lived in England; the eldest sister, May Brooks, lived in Australia.

May was very excited and sent a letter to Australia House acknowledging that she had heard indirectly of the discovery of her brother's grave. She wondered if it would be useful if she came over to France. However, although excited, May was the first to express doubts about the find; realising what little of her brother's remains would be left and how difficult it would be to make a positive identification, she wrote: 'If only one could be sure, it sounds rather hopeless after four years.'[6]

In March 1920 Smith called at Australia House again. Major Phillips was absent, attending the inquiry in France, and Smith once again discussed the matter with Sam MacMillan. Smith told him that James Burns had requested his nephew be present at the exhumation to make sure the body found was indeed Robert's. MacMillan let Smith know that this, in his view, would not present a problem and that permission would undoubtedly be granted.

Not much later Smith received another letter from Allen, informing him that he now believed that the said grave contained the remains of another deceased (probably British) officer. Smith thought this strange because the letter also stated that the remains had not yet been exhumed and that arranging this would take some time. How could the major be so sure it wasn't Robert's remains in that grave, Smith wondered?

When Major Phillips returned from the hearing in France, MacMillan told him about Smith's request to be allowed to be present when the exhumation was carried out. Phillips, much to MacMillan's surprise, reacted as if stung by a bee. Marching back into his office he immediate ordered his secretary to send a letter to Smith, informing him that he had been sadly misinformed by MacMillan.[7] Phillips refused Smith permission to be present, explaining that it would be useless to attend because 'after the lapse of such a long period and with all badges, identification discs, papers, trinkets and all possible sources of identity having been removed, it was, at this late stage, a matter of practical impossibility to identify a body'.[8]

When Smith visited Australia House after receiving Phillips' letter, Phillips explained that he could do nothing else but refuse his presence at the exhumation. The English exhumation teams refused to allow any civilians to be present and, because they were in charge of exhumation procedures, Phillips had no authority to overrule this. MacMillan overheard the conversation and told one of the secretaries that this was a blatant lie.[9] After a small incident, where a civilian had fainted after attending the exhumation of a son, the English had become more careful about blocking exhumations from view by putting up a screen.

MacMillan was aware that a request to be allowed to attend would need to go through official channels but that most requests were granted. MacMillan himself had been present at a large number of exhumations with family members attending. General Griffiths, commander of the AIF, had always endorsed and sanctioned MacMillan's policy of permitting the attendance of fathers, mothers and any other close adult relatives at reinterments. MacMillan knew there was nothing out of the ordinary about Smith's request, but he suspected there was something out of the ordinary about Phillips' refusal.

Phillips later phoned Smith at his hotel and assured him that all precautions and care would be taken when the grave was opened, and that his own men would make all possible identifications once the remains were unearthed. Phillips told Smith to sit back and be patient. The AGS would get back to him as soon as possible.

But Smith was not about to sit back. The major's unexpected refusal, along with Allen's previous letter, planted a seed of doubt in his mind. He could not fathom Phillips' almost hostile refusal to let him attend the exhumation—unless there was something to hide perhaps?

His sense that the two most notable men in the AGS, Phillips and Allen, were giving him the run-around grew as events took a turn for the worse during the next few weeks.[10] But for now, he decided that he would not bow to the wishes of Major Phillips. If need be he would go to the highest authority to gain permission to see for himself if the body in the opened grave was actually his wife's cousin's. This was James Burns's wish and Cecil Smith was not prepared to let anything get in the way of this, unless it was completely unavoidable.

Chapter 16
THE ALLEGED HOAX

It was mid-1920 and in Australia snippets of conflicting information about the Australian Graves Services in France had been finding their way into the newspapers. A number of articles that put the AGS in a bad light were published at the beginning of 1920, but there was also good news. John Oxenham arrived in Australia with his heroic story about the Australian major who found the bodies of missing men when nobody else was able to. The Australian Graves Services, very much under scrutiny, could well use some positive news in its midst, so Senator Pearce was undoubtedly pleased when Oxenham's story made it into print.

Headlines in bold revealed a story about a very special Australian working for the AGS in France. He was a 'finder of missing men', the newspapers delightedly announced, bravely scouring the countryside by himself in an effort to find the missing loved ones of Australia's bereaved.[1] The photos used to illustrate these articles showed Allen as a somewhat jovial and assuring fellow; the information that this amiable, God-fearing man did not drink or swear, and was held in high esteem by his men, did a lot to set at rest the minds of those who had questioned the functioning of the AGS.

It was around this time that General Birdwood left Australia and crossed the ocean to visit the Australian Graves Services in France. In France, he mostly spoke with the English officers there, but they assured him there was no truth to the claim that the AGS was flawed. There had been some problems in the past with the Australians, the English told Birdwood, but the Australians had assured them that it had all been dealt with. In an interview with the press Birdwood was quick to send back word that, as far as he could see, all matters concerning the AGS were going according to plan. After a difficult period, during which it had been forced to deal with start-up problems, the service now appeared to be running smoothly under the leadership of Major Phillips in London, Captain Meikle in Villers-Bretonneux and the man Birdwood had come to know as Major Allen in Poperinghe.

Although the general had not personally met Allen during his visit, an English officer, Colonel Francis Sutton, had given him a most excellent and unsolicited testimonial of the major's work. Sutton assured him that all was going well in Poperinghe, praising Allen and his team. But after inspecting a number of cemeteries, the tone of Birdwood's first, almost jubilant commentaries became more cautious. To the press Birdwood continued to express his satisfaction with the manner in which the Australians tended to the graves of their dead. He did, however, foresee problems and let the public know that, owing to the magnitude of the task, he did not expect the work to be completed within two years. The cemeteries now appeared unkempt, he said, but he trusted that all would soon be in perfect order. He asked the public to have patience.[2]

A few days after the article about Birdwood's visit to France made newspaper headlines, a letter was published in the Melbourne *Age* claiming that again the public was being misled with falsely reassuring information: 'Rank growth of grass covers the majority of cemeteries, whilst in many, exposed to winds and weather the crosses have fallen, decayed and rotten since erection.' The letter was signed 'W. Lee ex Graves Services'.[3]

In the midst of all this, Alfred Allen now found himself under the scrutiny of the Burns family. He had let them know in a personal letter that he had made an extensive search of the Fromelles area. 'I traced where a cross had been removed, the inscription giving the exact date of death and was informed that a British officer had been "lifted" by the Germans and removed but no one knew where and after a further search I discovered this cross at Fournes cemetery, the only cross of its kind with the date of death and the word "Fromelles" on the cross,' he wrote. But 'none of these crosses mention any names,'[4] so he could not be sure who was buried there. The Germans had not recognised the difference between Australians and Brits during the war. For them, the two appeared very similar; Allen thought that although the Germans had said that British soldiers were buried in the area, the grave could just as easily contain Australians.

Allen did not explain why the Germans would go to the trouble of digging up the grave of an enemy just to bury it in another place. It did not appear to have any logic to it, Smith thought. When asked about it, Allen told Smith that people in the village had told him about the reinterment of that particular grave.

During the war, because of their close proximity to the battlefront, these small French villages had been completely deserted. Civilians had taken what they could and left. Who had told Allen about the reburial by the Germans and why had this person not left like everyone else? Smith slowly began to suspect the information might not be altogether true. The major, however, assured him: 'I followed up by going to a Graves Recovery Unit officer of that District, who put a GRU strip on that cross. I asked him if he knew what bodies were under the cross; he said he did not know. No one ever touched this cross. I have every reason to think this is the cross previously referred to [by the Germans].'[5]

Smith did not know what to think of the somewhat muddled information he was getting. As he had nothing else to go by, he would, at least for the time being, go along with Allen's information. But the feeling that he needed to be present when the grave was opened grew stronger day by day. Losing faith in the authorities, Smith decided that he and only he would be the one making sure that the remains lying in that particular grave in Fournes were those of Robert Burns. Smith had heard so many conflicting arguments while inquiring into his wife's cousin's case, it could be no one else's call. He was beyond the point where he would take anyone's word for it.

Smith had known Robert for years and he was certain that he would be able to identify the remains. If there was just a tuft of hair left or some skin, Smith would know; Robert had more than one distinctive feature. No matter how deteriorated Robert's corpse was, Cecil Smith was more than certain that he would probably be the only person present at the exhumation who would be able to make a positive identification of the body. Having been refused by Major Phillips, he would, however, need to take other steps to ensure that he would actually be allowed to take a look at the remains when they were lifted from the grave.

Despite all the emerging rumours and difficulties he was having in regard to the Burns case, Alfred Allen kept his eye on what was important. While Birdwood was still in France, Allen managed to maintain his reputation as a skilled body diviner by unexpectedly locating the remains of an Australian hero. The soldier's father had recently visited Poperinghe in search of his son's grave and, like Smith, had asked Allen for help. Allen had not been able to locate the son's gravesite at the time and the father had been forced to return to London, disillusioned at having to go back without closure.

Against all odds, Allen managed to find the son's grave at another gravesite just outside Fournes-en-Weppes. The discovery came just one day before the father was to return to Australia. After being intercepted in London and informed of the discovery of the location of his son's grave, the father cancelled his trip back to Australia. Allen assured the father that the grave contained the corpse of his son, an Australian Victoria Cross holder.

His ribbon had been found after exhumation, as well as his identity disc. This distinguished soldier's father had proceeded to Belgium just in time to witness the internment of his son's remains in a cemetery. Birdwood, still in the country, forwarded this tale to the Australian newspapers, which published the story about the remarkable find.[6] In November Senator Pearce thanked General Birdwood for his reassuring messages from France.[7]

Not in any way intending to give up, Smith in the meantime went back to Australia House and talked to MacMillan again. Smith expressed his indignation at the curt letter he had received from Major Phillips, refusing him permission to attend the exhumation. MacMillan listened as Smith once again explained his desire to be present, if only for the 'old man's sake'. MacMillan knew Smith would not yield and secretly cheered him on. This man was not acting out of a misplaced obstinacy; his resolve came from a deep sense of obligation towards the family. MacMillan suspected that nothing would hold Smith back and he would do what he could to help. Smith would be present if he had to disguise himself as one of the exhumers to do so, he told MacMillan.

Major Phillips overheard the two men talking in the corridor and confronted Smith about this.[8] Smith, unfazed by the sudden appearance of Phillips, repeated his protest and wanted to know why Phillips was making such a song and dance about the whole thing. Major Phillips curtly repeated his former decision, confirming that he would not tolerate the attendance of civilians at exhumations. Not now, and not ever.

Smith, just as tenacious and motivated to do what Phillips was trying to prevent, let the major know that he was not motivated by any idle or morbid curiosity, and that he was truly concerned about a possible mix-up if he let anyone else do the identifying. He literally begged Phillips for permission to attend the exhumation.

This was as low as he was prepared to stoop, but Phillips remained resolute and all Smith could do was leave. But he would not back down.

Chapter 17

CROSSING THE CHANNEL

When Smith returned once again to Australia House at the beginning of May, he bumped into Sergeant Michael Skelton there. After Skelton was introduced to him as one of Allen's junior staff, who was usually based at Poperinghe, Smith thought it might be helpful to explain his predicament to the seemingly sympathetic officer. He let Skelton know that Allen had allegedly found evidence that Robert was buried in a grave at Fournes, but had changed his mind about the location very soon afterward. Allen, since then, had reverted to his original conclusion—he now believed that Burns's remains were most likely in the grave at Fournes and he was in the process of arranging an exhumation. Major Phillips, for some unfathomable reason, refused Smith permission to attend this upcoming exhumation. Smith told Skelton how sad and frustrating the whole affair had become to him.

Smith and Skelton chatted about the possibility of marking the grave, if it were the correct one. Smith asked if it might be possible to place a white fence around it. He had seen graves with such a white fence in France and thought it would be an appropriate way to mark Robert's last resting place. Smith casually inquired about the cost of such a fence and went on to ask if there would be any objection if his wife's cousin's grave were ornamented with nice German brass shells. Of course, Smith would meet any costs involved directly to Skelton.[1] Skelton declined to tell Smith that all graves were uniformly established and that there could be no question of placing any fancy ornaments or decorative fence-work.

A few days later Smith sent a letter to Skelton reminding him of their conversation and casually asked the sergeant if it would be possible to forward any information he picked up about the exhumation, especially any definite dates. Smith, by now certain that any efforts he made to attend the proceedings in France might well be frustrated by Phillips and Allen, told Skelton that if he forwarded the dates Smith could arrange to be present by 'accident'.[2] It was a crafty scheme, but by now Smith was running out of options and he realised he was up against clever opponents.

Reading the letter, Skelton was beginning to doubt his involvement with Smith. He felt he was slowly being lured into a compromising position. Just weeks previously he had been called up to give evidence about the conflict between Lee and Kingston at the first AGS inquiry. Sitting in that room with the members of the court had made him feel very uncomfortable. Kingston had been his OC when he joined the unit at Villers-Bretonneux in September and he had tried to avoid saying anything incriminating about Kingston when he was called up to testify. But the mood had changed dramatically when the members of the court implied that Skelton had slept with an elderly prostitute on the chateau's grounds. According to Skelton, this was all a lie that Will Bollen had spread around.

As Skelton told it, one evening he had attended a concert given by the German prisoners of war. It was held in a camp nearby and it was there he met an older lady, who was around 55 years old, and her two daughters. Skelton and a couple of others had taken the women to an estaminet across the road from the camp and had enjoyed a few drinks with them. After an hour or so, Skelton had left the bar and was in bed by eleven o'clock that evening, he told the court. He had gone to bed alone.

The following day he had bumped into the women again in the chateau's grounds and politely bid them good day. He explained to the court that he was a married man and that his wife was staying in England.[3] When asked if Kingston had been seen accompanying the women, he told them he could not remember. He did not want to get into trouble and he certainly did not want to incriminate Kingston. After the hearing he had scurried away and, when a list of the names of those to be discharged and sent back to Australia became known, he had been very relieved that his name was not on the list and that he had only been ordered to work from a new location, Poperinghe.

Smith's letter now felt like a new test of his loyalty and something that could potentially drag him into another conflict. Thankful that he had got off leniently before, Skelton really did not want to get into any trouble. He especially did not want to be sent back to Australia prematurely, as the other men had been.

The job he was doing was, in a strange way, pleasant and fulfilling. Poperinghe, where he was now based, was as good a place as any to be; at home in Australia no one questioned his motives for staying abroad. His parents could boast about how their son was still carrying out a noble job and he could visit his wife in England once a month when he was on leave. It was a happy arrangement for Skelton and so, in an effort to keep his record clean and his superiors happy, he confided in his OC, Alfred Allen. Showing his superior the letter he had received brought on a sense of relief for Skelton. But, confronted with Smith's scheming, Allen in turn talked to Major Phillips about it.

Phillips reacted furiously, because Smith had once again attempted to bypass him. Phillips phoned Smith and did not hide his annoyance. Smith then came to Australia House and assured the major that it had not been his intention to sidestep him but that he had befriended Skelton as a last resort. It had become a matter of principle for him to attend the exhumation, Smith said, and he made it clear that he did not trust Phillips—or Allen, for that matter. He believed that, for some inexplicable reason, the two of them were teaming up to prevent him from witnessing what would emerge from the grave.

The conversation soon turned nasty and the two men accused each other of contemptible behaviour.[4] Finally Smith left the office red-faced and highly exasperated, leaving in his wake a very annoyed Major Phillips.

Still hoping for a positive outcome, Smith, after he had calmed down, returned to Australia House later that day and spoke to Colonel Hogben's official secretary. The secretary told him that he would ask the colonel if Smith could apply for special permission through the Imperial War Office to attend the exhumation. When Hogben returned, his secretary explained about Smith's request and, unaware of the dispute between Phillips and Smith, Hogben rang Fabian Ware's office the next day.[5]

Hogben inquired if the English had special rules in place about having a civilian present at an exhumation and Ware's secretary explained that permission was not always granted, because in some cases it was not advisable to have civilians attending the exhumation. This was especially so when small children or elderly people applied to be present, but the secretary could see no reason why it should be refused in this case. He would inquire with Ware about the matter, he said. In the end, it was the great man himself who finally gave his approval.

When Phillips heard that Smith had gone over his head once again in his quest to gain approval, putting his request directly to Hogben, this caused the smouldering fire to flare up. By now the whole matter had got completely out of hand and had become a matter of principle for both men. Phillips was especially annoyed with Hogben for not consulting with him first. It felt like a breach of trust on his superior's part. MacMillan later told the court that the enraged Phillips had come to him shouting that 'he wasn't the man to be beaten by Hogben'.[6] MacMillan realised the whole matter was spiralling out of control and that the argument was no longer about who would be more able to identify a body. It had turned into a fight about who was going to get his way.

Hogben, still unaware of any dispute, promised Smith that he would get at least two days' notice before the exhumation took place in France. Hogben recommended that Smith, when he received news, should proceed to Hazebrouck, a town in northern France near Dunkirk. The colonel himself would arrange for a car to pick him up there. Smith was so relieved he almost hugged the colonel; he did, however, tell him of his fears of possibly being sidetracked by Phillips and Allen. But Hogben was surprised by Smith's doubts. Hearing about these difficulties for the first time, he waved Smith's anxieties away, reassuring him that any qualms he might have were surely based on a misunderstanding.

That afternoon MacMillan bumped into Warrant Officer James Rolston, who told him that Phillips had personally handed him a private letter addressed to Major Alfred Allen.[7] Rolston was instructed by Phillips to see to it that the letter was dispatched immediately, but the warrant officer had secretly read the letter before he sent it off. He had been suspicious about the large numbers of AIF men that Phillips was replacing with civilians and MPs, and wanted to know what was going on between the major in Poperinghe and the one in London.

The letter wasn't about replacements at all but about an exhumation. The message urged Allen to get the exhumation done immediately, before Smith would have a chance to cross the Channel.[8] MacMillan wasn't surprised. They discussed how much the AGS was turning into a military police unit. They both harboured the same feeling when it came to how Phillips was running the show. Rolston let MacMillan know that he could no longer associate himself with this kind of charade and that he was in the course of applying for a discharge. Rolston left the service on his own request just a month later.

For the next few days Smith waited for the notice about the impending exhumation to arrive, but then he began to doubt that he would ever hear anything. He felt he needed to take matters into his own hands. By now totally fed up, he was in doubt as to who could and could not be trusted, so he crossed over to Ostend in Belgium on Sunday, 16 May 1920, without letting anyone except Skelton know in advance that he would be coming. Although Skelton had betrayed him previously, he felt the man had been courteous to him and been sympathetic and understanding of his point of view. Skelton was the only person on the mainland he could turn to for help. Stressing to Skelton to keep mum about his arrival, that evening Smith reached Poperinghe, where Skelton had booked him a room at the Skindles Hotel. Skelton had let Smith know that the exhumation was imminent and that arrangements were already in place in France. But it soon dawned on Smith that Skelton was not to be trusted.

The Skindles was actually a classic guesthouse that had been built in the eighteenth century and had been given its name by the Brits during the war. Across the road the British had also opened an officers' club bearing the same name. After the Armistice, the hotel and club had become the place to stay for high-ranking officers and visitors with enough money. Smith decided he would confront Allen with his unexpected presence the next morning.

The next morning on Monday, 17 May, he immediately paid Allen a surprise visit at his Bird Cage Camp office. Allen appeared very startled when Smith made his entrance demanding to know if the exhumation had already been done or if it was still in the pipeline.

Smith saw how, slowly, Allen regained his composure. The major, fumbling for words, inquired whether a date in three days' time on Thursday, 20 May would do. Smith, happy to finally get things under way with a definite day, agreed and left the office with a smile on his face.

What Smith did not know then was that Allen had already made an arrangement with the British exhumers for the following day, 18 May, to open the grave at Fournes.[9] The Australian Graves Services always had to put in a request to the British Graves Registration Unit if they wanted a location dug up or an existing grave opened. The British exhumers had already confirmed Allen's request and, realising the predicament that had emerged, Allen that evening hurriedly sent word to the GRU for the exhumation to be cancelled. Setting a date of 20 May would give Allen another two days to consult with Phillips about the course of action to be taken. Although Allen denied this was the case when later questioned about it.

However, the British exhumers did not receive Allen's postponement message on time and proceeded to the site at Fournes the next morning.[10] They waited, standing around for an hour, wondering if the Australians would show up; the actual digging could only begin when the Australians had authorised the spot. A few hours later they packed it all in and left, supposing that someone must have made a mistake.

Phillips was furious when Skelton told him the next day that Smith had secretly made his way to Belgium in an attempt to prevent the exhumation taking place without him being present. Phillips had let Smith know that arrangements would be made for his attendance in due course and he was to stay in London until the details had been provided to him.

Phillips, fuming that Smith once again had taken no notice of his advice and had elected to proceed under his own steam, sent Allen a personal letter. He first dictated the letter to his secretary, who in turn typed it and then gave it to Warrant Officer Rolston to dispatch. It let Allen know that he should try to avoid Smith being present at the exhumation and that Allen should ask for proof that Smith had been granted permission to attend. Hogben's secretary had told Phillips that Ware's approval had not come as a written document but had been passed on by word of mouth. Without any papers, Smith would not have a leg to stand on.

Allen always denied having received any such letter from Phillips, although he told Smith that the Brits wouldn't give him permission to be present when they opened the grave.[11] If Smith did not hold written proof or some form of document that gave him authorisation, Allen simply could not allow his attendance. Having come so far and being promised just two days before that he would be able to attend, Smith did not even try to argue with Allen. He went straight to Colonel Sutton, the British OC. Smith had no time to waste; it was just a day before the Brits would start digging up the grave.

Sutton handed Smith written permission without a thought and appeared surprised to hear of the difficulties the Australians were presenting.[12] The colonel asked Smith if he had been the cause of a delay a couple of days earlier. Smith did not know what Sutton was talking about, but when the colonel explained that his exhumation team had waited at Fournes for hours on 18 May for Allen to show up, Smith could only give him a surprised stare. It appeared that Allen had cancelled the appointment on Monday evening, but the telegram had not reached them on time.

It was the first Smith had heard about the postponed exhumation. He was stupefied that Allen had set a date before he had arrived and this increased his feeling that something was very wrong. If he had arrived at Poperinghe two days later, the exhumation would have been carried out without him. No one had bothered to inform him or send him a telegram, and by now he knew for certain that no one ever would have done so.

Sutton went on to explain that his men had not received the message in time and that Allen had set a new date, but Sutton could not guarantee Smith that his men could do the exhumation the next day. It would be a tight call. He advised Smith to call back that afternoon to make sure the date and time of the exhumation were as now planned.

That afternoon Smith finally got confirmation. The grave would be opened the following day, Thursday. The working party provided by the British to carry out the exhumation was there as well as Major William Busby of the Australian Red Cross, who Smith had met on the boat crossing the Channel and to whom he had explained his difficulties. Staff Sergeant Thomas Rowe and another officer from Poperinghe stood in solemn silence and anticipation as the diggers gathered their tools and waited for Rowe's orders. Everyone was there except Major Alfred Allen. He had suddenly reported himself sick, a case of typhoid fever. The major was in hospital, Rowe awkwardly explained to Smith. He had been admitted that morning and was not able to attend.[13]

Smith, now very suspicious about any difficulties raised concerning the grave and its contents, could not help but wonder if Allen's illness might have something to do with what they would find once the grave revealed its contents. If it was to happen without Alfred Allen's presence, so be it, Smith thought. Rowe showed the men the cross that marked the spot they were to exhume. The men went to work digging up the soil under the cross as Smith held his breath. In regard to the work of exhuming a body, the diggers were warned not to dig too close to a body but to stay just outside the grave. The precaution prevented the body from being disturbed and more importantly revealed if more than one body was buried in the same spot.

As the men continued to carefully dig deeper Smith realised that whatever the outcome the result would not be good. If the grave did not contain Robert's remains, it would be a blow to the old man and his daughters; but if it did, it would be equally distressing. It would confirm that Robert was dead.

After a considerable time, the men looked at Smith. Shaking his head, one man said: 'It appears to be empty.' [14] Although he had been sceptical from the start, this was still a big let-down for Smith. He knew it would prove an even greater disappointment for James Burns.

One man started prodding the earth to one side of the hole and came across some cloth. Hoping to find at least something, the working crew started digging at this spot. Smith watched as the party went to work in an expert and very careful way. He had heard from the Australians many demeaning remarks about the British exhumers; they were supposed to be slack and their work left much to be desired. What Smith witnessed that day was something totally different from anything he had heard. That afternoon the exhumation party uncovered one British officer and four soldiers, all Brits, buried in the German part of the cemetery in a location next to the cross Allen had indicated.

Smith was surprised that they had been able to find anything at all. He suspected the grave would be empty or at best be holding a bag stuffed with straw to make it look like a body or body parts. He had heard of such things happening. The Australians accused the Brits of such methods.[15] Over time, what had begun as a lax system had grown more and more vulnerable to abuse. The English had started paying a premium for every body found; this resulted in bodies being dismembered and the parts offered as the partial remains of more than one soldier. There had been insufficient supervision and the officers who had been picked to organise and oversee this work appeared to fall short. When these practices became known the premium was promptly abolished. Still, there were rumours that sometimes graves had been established without actually holding a body.

As the bodies surfaced, Rowe and the Brits identified the corpses by their buttons and other markings; none of them were Australian and none of them could have been Lieutenant Robert Burns. The English told Smith they were going to dig up the whole row just in case. If there were more British soldiers there, they themselves would want to know; if any Australians were found, they would inform the Australian Graves Services and also pass on the information directly to Smith.

Smith thanked the men. They had done their work well and, although he felt deflated because it had all been in vain, he was satisfied that these men at least had done what they had promised.

Rowe explained to Smith that he had been lucky to be able to attend, because the English had recently applied new rules after a lady who had come looking for her son fainted at the sight of the corpse. Ever since they had placed hessian screens around the working parties at the sites and had forbidden civilians to be present. Somehow Smith did not feel as lucky as Rowe thought he should.

Chapter 18
SAM MacMILLAN

Fed up with the way Major Phillips was handling the Burns case, Sam MacMillan wrote a letter of complaint to Senator Pearce who had first been appointed as minister for defence in Andrew Fisher's Labor government of 1908 and had continued in that role right through Billy Hughes' long prime ministership. In his sworn statement of 19 November 1920, MacMillan explained about the hoaxing and the treachery to which Cecil Smith had been subjected during his search for Robert Burns's missing body,[1] how Major Phillips and Major Allen had worked together in an attempt to keep Smith out of their way. MacMillan had always had his doubts regarding the remarkable 'finds' of Allen and he would have not been at all surprised if the grave had turned up empty. In fact, he had written a letter to Robert Burns's sister, May Brooks, expressing his doubts about a possible find in April 1920. 'There is no reason to believe your brother is buried in the German Cemetery at Fournes,' he wrote.[2] He went on to explain in his letter to Senator Pearce how impossible it was to identify a body after such a lapse of time, particularly if trinkets and other sources of identification had been removed.

MacMillan described how the press, with help from Phillips and Allen, had accused the British of 'loose methods' and how Allen had accused the British exhumers of cutting bodies in half to up the body count.[3] MacMillian was aware that when the British started paying an extra half a crown for every body found, some of the men resorted to such methods. Even the French, who started searching their fields in the hope of finding a body, were known to up the count in a dubious manner. There were also exhumation units who were obsessed with the idea that their reputation depended on discovering the greatest possible number of bodies in the shortest possible time, and this resulted in many graves without names and sometimes with names but without bodies.

Allen and Phillips claimed that the Brits were often not able to identify an Australian corpse. MacMillan was surprised by Allen's claim that the experienced Brits were apparently unable to establish an identity when Allen himself was able to do so immediately. All 150 graves in Poperinghe were provided with a name. It was the only cemetery in the whole area without 'unknown soldiers'. There was something going on and it had to do with the identification of bodies. How was it possible that Allen found them and was then able to identify most of the bodies on the spot? MacMillan, indignant and appalled, wrote: 'The thing is preposterous and must and will be exposed however much it goes against the grain to disillusion the bereaved.'[4]

In his letter to Senator Pearce, Sam MacMillan included a copy of a letter Phillips had sent to Allen on 15 May. It began:

Dear Allen,

Shortly after leaving this office, this morning on your return trip to France our mutual friend Mr Smith again visited this office and gave me the opportunity of telling him that I strongly objected to the procedure he adopted with regard to his recent communication to Skelton. He, of course, expressed his sorrow and stated that he did not mean anything by going over my head even though my letter disallowing his presence in France had been received . . . I am now directed [by Hogben] much against my will to put all facilities at Mr Smith's disposal . . .

Phillips ended his letter with:

For God's sake have it carried out immediately if at all possible, and then advise me that the exhumation has been completed. This may not be possible, but you understand the position, and you can quite see that I do not wish to suffer this loss of dignity when it refers to a man whose principles are certainly rather doubtful.

The letter was signed, 'Yours in confidence.'[5]

MacMillan hoped that this letter would prove that Phillips and Allen had been scheming together. Phillips had written another letter to Allen on that same day; this one was an official letter, conveying Hogben's orders to give full cooperation to Smith. But this letter containing Hogben's orders was not posted immediately. Phillips had delayed transmitting his instructions for 24 hours, hoping that Allen would immediately act on the private letter and get the exhumation done before Smith could get across.

MacMillan told how Smith, when crossing the Channel, had run into Major William Busby of the Australian Red Cross, who was on the same steamer and was well acquainted with Allen.[6] After listening to Smith's story, Busby paid a visit to Allen at Poperinghe and demanded to know what was going on. Allen explained that he had been nothing but helpful to Smith, and it was not his fault that Smith was not allowed to attend the exhumation. He thought Smith had no reason at all to be as annoyed as he appeared to be. Phillips and he had been quite courteous towards the man and it was not their fault that the Brits did not allow civilians to attend an exhumation.

MacMillan was informed that Allen reported sick on the day of the exhumation. MacMillan thought Allen's claimed illness must have been an attempt to avoid Smith, so as not to have to face any awkward questions.

Sam MacMillan did not inform Senator Pearce of the means by which he had obtained a copy of the highly revealing private letter Phillips had sent to Allen.

Chapter 19
WILLIAM JAMES FOSTER
December 1920

Was there a hoaxing of bodies going on? If so, Senator Pearce wanted to get to the bottom of it. The whole sordid situation in France was getting out of hand and Pearce demanded action.[1] He had written to London asking for a transcript of the proceedings of the previous court inquiry concerning Lee and Kingston to be sent to him but he had not received anything. An urgent telegram advising those responsible in France to send the papers as soon as possible was delivered to Australia House in November 1920.

Lee had alleged impropriety at those proceedings and Pearce wanted to read for himself how much of this was true. Pearce also urged Fisher to hold a new inquiry, this time into the alleged hoaxing in the Lieutenant Burns case. He suggested the inquiry be presided by Lieutenant Colonel McFarlane.

Percy Muir McFarlane had an impeccable record and was held in high esteem by General Birdwood, but McFarlane himself politely refused this appointment.[2] His reasons were that he had previously made an unofficial verbal report to the AIF 'that was unfavourable to Lieutenant Lee in which he had stated that in his opinion Lee was unsuited for the position he occupied at Amiens'.[3]

There was also a matter concerning a protracted dispute about McFarlane receiving a medal for his services during the war. Birdwood had proposed it, but the high commissioner, Andrew Fisher, as well as other military authorities opposed it, believing that a number of soldiers had showed as much if not more courage than McFarlane and were perhaps more deserving of a medal. McFarlane had been injured lightly in the first weeks of the war and had hardly seen combat.[4] Besides, as Fisher pointed out, the recommendation had come too late.

McFarlane, notified by Pearce about the trouble in France, deemed it advisable to avoid any conflict of interest. Although he had been granted the Victory Medal in the end, it had not come about without a scuffle. Fisher and he had got off on the wrong foot and he had openly vented his opinion about Lee in the months the first court inquiry was held, so he did not think he should be the one to preside over the hearing. Besides, he had been offered a job on the staff at the Royal Military College Sandhurst in Camberley.

Pearce, although disappointed, understood McFarlane's decision. He turned to Fisher for advice. In his letter to Fisher, Pearce also recommended that Phillips be suspended, at least until the inquiry was over. He also urged utmost discretion in the case and he wanted Lee's allegations reassessed.

Fisher tried to convince Pearce that a court of inquiry was

in no way called for; an informal inquiry would be sufficient in this case. MacMillan's word, Fisher claimed, was not to be relied on.[5] He had some serious questions to answer, and as for Lee—well, the man had had his say.

Fisher had personally inquired into Smith's complaints and he could see nothing that validated what he was claiming. Phillips was a very trustworthy and efficient officer with an impeccable record, Fisher wrote, and he did not think it advisable to suspend Phillips before he was even charged with any wrongdoing. A suspension might raise questions. If Pearce was really resolute in his decision to proceed then Fisher proposed an investigation performed by AIF officers.

Pearce answered that he wanted an official inquiry and he wanted a court composed as much as possible of permanent officers, but none from the Australian Graves Services. He insisted that Phillips be relieved from duty until the hearing was over, and that came about on 23 November 1920.

Fisher let Pearce know that the proceedings of the first inquiry had been sent to the judge advocate-general, Felix Cassel, and they were waiting for his review of the proceedings. As soon as Cassel had put his findings to paper, Pearce would receive a transcript of the proceedings and findings.

—•—

In the meantime, Fisher's military advisor, Colonel Percy Buckley, had set to work to find three men qualified to be members of the inquiry board. His first choice as president was William James Foster.

After starting his career as a teacher, Foster had joined the army in 1906 and been promoted to lieutenant in the Light Horse Brigade the following year. He was promoted to temporary captain on 1 February 1912 and in October 1913 he went to New Zealand on exchange duty. There he became a brigade major of the 4th Brigade (Newcastle). When World War I broke out, he joined the Australian Imperial Forces as a captain and aide-de-camp. His battalion sailed for Egypt in October 1914.

He'd seen some action, but he'd also held staff positions; although his progress in the military had been steady, it had not been in any way spectacular. Foster had never held a command in the field and was not known for holding rigid views about sticking to the rules and regulations: he believed in getting the job done, and if that meant bending a few procedures, well, so be it. Maybe that was the reason he was chosen. His career had been reasonably uneventful, but his military record was impeccable.[6]

Buckley knew that Foster's wife, Margaret, had died just months before and in some ways Foster was still mourning her death. Margaret had been a nurse in the AIF when he met her and she had served in Egypt and later in England. After meeting in London they'd returned to Australia in 1919 to marry in Sydney. She'd died in childbirth, leaving him with a son. During the war, the Light Horse Brigade had brought Foster to Gallipoli where he'd seen men maimed, suffering from terrible wounds; he'd heard their cries as they called out for their mothers in the throes of death and he'd seen them lose their minds as they sat in their trenches waiting for the enemy to advance. He later recalled that nothing had pained or saddened him as much as waiting helplessly at the hospital while doctors tried to save his wife and son.

After Margaret's death, Foster joined the staff of the Royal Military College at Camberley in England, occupying a desk job. He had no idea how to take care of an infant so, when a position in England had been offered to him, he'd left his son behind in Australia in the care of Margaret's sister.

The request from Buckley and Fisher for him to preside at the forthcoming inquiry came as a surprise to Foster; without any legal experience, he did not really consider himself a suitable candidate. But having been personally approached by the highest-ranking men at Australia House, Foster was well aware of the importance of the request and he ultimately acceded to it.

He soon learned how desperate they were. Accusations of misconduct, negligence and hoaxing had been voiced by numerous men. A previous inquiry, partly held in France and partly in England, had come up with no valid grounds for the accusations, but a number of men were, nevertheless, discharged and sent home. One of them, Lieutenant William Lee, had subsequently begun sending accusatory letters to the minister for defence, Senator Pearce. Lee accused the members of the previous inquiry board in France and England of being bribed and was making a whole spectacle of it, threatening to go to the press to reveal the story if nothing was done about it. It was Foster's mission to get to the bottom of matters and hopefully calm things down.

To make up the panel for the inquiry, Buckley asked Foster if he had any capable men in mind to serve as members of the court. Foster recommended Beavis and Whitham. Young Leslie Ellis Beavis was a man with a respectable record: in 1916 he'd been sent to Egypt at the age of 21, and by the time he was 22 he had already become a major. Fighting at Ypres in Belgium, he had sustained gas attacks and the effects had forced him to evacuate to England. Thirty nine-year-old Lieutenant Colonel John Lawrence Whitham had also served in Egypt and fought at Ypres.

Because the members of the previous inquiry board had been accused of having been bribed, everyone involved had taken particular care to pick men with impeccable records, who were not in any way attached, or had any ties to, the former AGD or the AGS and had no knowledge of the earlier proceedings. Pearce had specifically wanted the president and the members to be as impartial and as unprejudiced as possible. He did not want a repeat of the last inquiry. The people that Buckley and Fisher had sought out were untainted by any wrongdoing and Buckley vouched for all three.

They were to address the matter without prejudice. Senator Pearce had especially wanted the issue surrounding the hoaxing of a body to be fully investigated and sorted out. The accusations were becoming too serious to sweep under any carpet. What's more, the accusations had not only come from within the army but also from outside it.

As Foster and his colleagues were to learn, it involved a colonel's son.

Chapter 20
THE SECOND INQUIRY

The second court of inquiry commenced in December 1920.[1] Witnesses would be called in one by one and the proceedings were to be kept as secret as possible. After taking the testimonies, Foster was to come to some kind of conclusion about what had gone on concerning Lieutenant Burns remains. It would be a hard nut to crack.

If he found substantial wrongdoing it would result in a referral for an official court martial. An army man at heart, Foster did not want to bring great disgrace and shame upon the good name, fame and reputation of Australia. Especially not on its military personnel. If he could, he would find a way around the ugly parts.

He realised that there were few people in the Australian Graves Services with more expertise and knowledge of its functioning than Majors Allen and Phillips. They had helped set up the service for the past year. If they were to be found guilty of any impropriety, the evidence would need to be undeniable and beyond any doubt.

Together with Beavis and Whitham, Foster set about the task of making a list of witnesses. The men called up to give evidence were all more or less friends of the accused. Witnesses were Colonel Sutton, who made no secret of his admiration for Allen; Warrant Officer Pitt, who had worked under Phillips at Australia House; Sergeant Rowe of Poperinghe, who had been present at the exhumation; Edward Lund, Phillips' personal driver and batman; Dorothy Doust, Phillips' secretary; Bill Meikle, whom Lee accused of being bribed during the previous inquiry and who was now working as officer in charge at Villers-Bretonneux; Captain Fennelly, a personal friend of Phillips; Brigadier General Jess, who had known Phillips since their time at the military academy in 1906; and Colonel Hogben.[2]

Cecil Arkell Smith was not called and Michael Skelton was also not approached to testify. It was planned that Lee, MacMillan and Bollen would be heard when the court was transferred to Australia. Pearce had let Fisher know that he wanted an additional inquest to take place in Australia so that the men who had been discharged could be heard.

Both Phillips and Allen were once more allowed to be present throughout the hearing and were given permission to put questions to witnesses and to call up any witnesses they desired. When Phillips additionally requested that his old friend Captain Fennelly, who had presided over the first inquiry, be present during the proceedings to support him, Foster refused.[3]

Although the court was mainly set up to inquire into the Robert Burns case, there were other matters to look into, including the alleged employment of Phillips' driver, Edward Lund, as part of his personal household while he was being paid by the AIF; Kingston, Lee and MacMillan had filed a complaint about this. The use of a personal AIF batman had been banned at the end of the war. Along with the financial reasons, the view was also taken that while wartime had justified the need for a batman, during peacetime it was not the AIF's task to equip their officers with a butler of sorts.

Rumours that Phillips and Allen were turning the AGS into a military police unit needed to be dealt with by the court. Percy Gray, one of the men who had been sent back to Australia after the first court inquiry, had written a letter to Senator Pearce saying he thought the 'so called Major Allen' should never have been put in charge.[4] Gray's argument was that the man had not done 'his bit' and his collaboration with Major Phillips, a former governor of a military gaol, had fed suspicions that the two were up to no good.

Speaking for the common soldiers, who despised the military police, Gray assumed Phillips would undoubtedly have many friends among the hated 'Jacks'. A lot of former MPs were always hanging around headquarters; they were in no way eager to return to Australia, and Gray said he thought they were most likely afraid of the payback they might receive back home. Gray had heard that Phillips was in the process of demobilising as many of the AGS staff as possible so as to replace them with military police. He was not only speaking for himself when he wrote that he'd 'much rather have the bones of his relatives rot in the open air than be handled by such men as the Military Police'.[5] He reckoned he was voicing the opinion of most of his comrades.

In Australia Lee was still writing one letter after another demanding a new hearing and inquiry. Lee alleged that Phillips and Allen had conspired together during the former inquiry and compromised the panel members by bribing them with jobs. This seemed to have some foundation when it became evident that just after the hearing Meikle had been made head of the department and MacLean, who had mouthed off about the deal, was suddenly sent home. Because of this, Pearce wanted the former case re-examined.

Foster was also to look into the matter of the sworn declaration sent to Senator Pearce by Sam MacMillan, which contained serious charges of maladministration taking place in the AGS in France and Belgium; MacMillan claimed that the identities of many graves were intentionally wrongly established over the period he was there. Pearce was taking these particular allegations very seriously.

The court assembled on 16 December 1920 in London at AIF headquarters. It was planned that at a later date it would reassemble in Australia to take evidence from those who had been discharged as a result of the first inquiry.

Major George Lort Phillips was the first to take the stand. He assured the court that he had been nothing but courteous to Cecil Arkell Smith and that he was very surprised to hear his attitude had been described as 'nasty' by that gentleman. When he had taken up his duties in February 1920 he had been informed that it was AGS policy that all exhumations be carried out by British army personnel only, and that visitors and civilians were to be excluded.[6]

In not permitting Smith to be present, he had only been conforming to an established rule. Phillips had witnessed many instances where, when graves had been opened, it was discovered that they contained the remains of someone other than the name on the headstone. He had also come across sacks in graves, stuffed to represent bodies, made up in the shape of a corpse. He blamed no one in particular for these tactics and did not explain whether the Australian Graves Services indulged in such methods.

Phillips claimed that Smith had created a certain amount of friction with all his actions; he had gone over Phillips' head and written to one of his sergeants without his knowledge in an effort to access inside information. Due to Smith's 'temperament', Phillips testified, he had been afraid that if any irregularities were uncovered during the exhumation, especially before they could be rectified, 'much unpleasantness would be caused'. This in turn would interfere with the unit's functioning.[7]

After weeks of harassing the AGS and everyone at Australia House, Smith had unexpectedly turned up in France. Phillips testified that he had first heard of Smith being present in France on 18 May, when Alfred Allen had notified him about it but this wasn't true. Skelton was the one who had informed him of Smith's plans and he in turn had hurriedly written a letter to Allen with instructions on how to proceed. Phillips did not explain why Smith had not been informed by himself or Allen about the exhumation previously planned on 18 May and why he had never received a notice beforehand. Phillips went on to state that he had never had any intention to mislead Smith in any way. He emphasised that he personally had no objection to any Australian civilian being present and that he had certainly never instructed Allen or any other person to mislead Smith in any way.

Phillips gave a very different account of how Smith and he parted ways after the heated discussion at Australia House. According to Phillips, after he had explained to Smith the reason for not being able to grant him the necessary facilities, Smith had said goodbye, shaken hands with him and left. Assuming the whole matter had been satisfactorily dealt with, Phillips carried on with his tasks and thought nothing more about it. Phillips said he had been very surprised when he heard that Smith had described the meeting as being 'highly unpleasant'.

The court might have been entitled to believe this if there had not been the small matter of the letter sent from Phillips to Major Allen in Poperinghe after he heard that Smith was on his way there. Dictated to his secretary on the evening of 15 May, the letter had urged Allen to get the exhumation done quickly, preferably without Smith's attendance. The last sentence in the letter translated from shorthand by Sam MacMillan read: 'for God's sakes get the job done, you know what is at stake.'[8]

Chapter 21
AN EMPTY GRAVE

Under oath, Alfred Allen once again told the court how he had scoured the countryside for any sign of Lieutenant Burns's grave. How he was informed that there were five mass graves holding British or Australian bodies at a spot called Pheasant Wood and that a British officer had been 'lifted' from a grave by the Germans and placed in another grave, but no one knew where. Major Allen explained that, to the Germans, Australians and British were pretty much of the same origin, therefore often, when the Germans gave information about any Allied graves, these were described as holding British soldiers.

In the course of the questioning it did not become clear who exactly had passed on the information of the reinterment of the British bodies, although Allen let the court know that he had got this information from the villagers. Why the Germans would go to the trouble of digging up a grave of an enemy only to bury it again a couple of miles down the road was another question left unexplained. Allen denied ever being aware of the existence of Mr Smith until Skelton showed him the letter Smith had written him. This was a lie: Allen had personally sent a letter to Smith in March informing him of his search in the area.

Later, after being called to the stand again, the major testified that on 11 May he had run into Mrs Smith at the railway station when returning to France from London. She told him that her husband would be proceeding to Belgium for the purpose of being present at the opening of the grave that was supposed to contain Lieutenant Burns's body.[1] Allen went on to state that he told her he did not know when the exhumation would take place. This did not seem to faze Mrs Smith in any way and she simply answered that her husband was determined to stay in France until it did.

Allen admitted that he had cancelled the opening of the Fournes grave for 18 May. His explanation of this was that Colonel Sutton had summoned him on that date about a visit to Ypres by Major Arthur Ingpen, who had been awarded an OBE and worked for the Imperial War Graves Commission, and the Belgian minister for interior Jules Renkin. Sutton had told Allen to cancel the exhumation at Fournes because the meeting at Ypres was much more important.

Ypres was almost demolished as a result of the war; architects and citizens had been invited to discuss how the town ought to be rebuilt. Some wanted to create a modern town, with the clean lines of the architecture of the day, but there were far more who would rather have the old town rebuilt in the Flemish medieval and Renaissance styles. It did not come as a surprise when the debate was ultimately won by the second option, which was promoted by Belgium's King Albert. Allen did not explain why his presence was so profoundly required at the 18 May meeting, but being an architect might have had something to do with it.

Strangely enough, when Sutton was later asked to testify, he could not remember either summoning Allen or directing him to meet up with Major Ingpen at Ypres. Sutton could remember himself meeting Ingpen and the minister at Ypres, although he could not recall Allen being there. However, the colonel did go on to say that he thought Major Allen was as good an officer as he had ever come across, and that the relatives in Australia should be very grateful for him being 'out all day trying to get identifications of bodies and he and his men are extraordinarily good' at it.[2]

Allen stuck to his story, claiming the matter he had discussed with Ingpen had been a very important one. He did not go into specifics about his visit, but he stressed that the exhumation had been put on hold for good reason. Smith, when he visited Allen's office had appeared visibly annoyed that he had not been notified about the exhumation. Allen explained that the note he had sent to Smith must have been held up in the post due to the weekend and he claimed that he had explained this to Smith. Allen was happy to set the exhumation for 20 May and could see no reason to refuse Smith attending, now he had a written letter from Colonel Sutton consenting to his presence.

Allen stressed that it was a terribly hard task to identify a body four years after it had been buried. The Germans, he said, dug long trenches and put the bodies in them in a disorderly fashion, one on top of the other, and then marked the trench with one cross.[3]

From his testimony, it became apparent that no one really wanted to open those mass graves. The stench was incredible and the bodies in an advanced state of decomposition. All of it turned into a tangle of limbs and rotten clothing. It was very hard to identify one body from another.

Phillips then was allowed to ask Allen a couple of questions. He wanted to know if Allen had received a personal letter from him. Allen replied that he had not. He had, however, received a telegram saying, 'Cancel personal letter, writing you.' But he did not have a clue what it referred to.

Both Phillips and Allen swore under oath that they had given Cecil Arkell Smith every assistance possible.

Chapter 22
STEALING NOTES

Asked to take the stand, Dorothy Doust, Major Phillips' secretary, reported that her notebook had been stolen.[1] It was taken just days after her boss had dictated a letter to her meant for Major Allen. She had transcribed her shorthand and sent the letter off to Allen on the same day, and then she had taken a break from work. When she returned to the office a few days later, her notebook was gone.

Doust said she had a pretty good idea who had nicked it—either Warrant Officer Wilkie or Sam MacMillan. She was surprised to hear that Allen had never received the letter that had been dictated to her and that she had passed on to Warrant Officer Rolston. She had no idea how this could be possible.

It was Warrant Officer Pritchard who had told her, when she came back from her leave, that he had seen MacMillan nosing through her notebook a number of times while she was gone. Wilkie and MacMillan were always after anything confidential,

Doust let the court know, and she suspected them both of the theft. She never locked the drawer because she thought it wasn't necessary. Although some of her notes were confidential, all were written in Pitman shorthand and there were not many people who could read it. She knew Warrant Officer Wilkie would not be able to read them, but she was pretty sure that MacMillan could.

She suspected that Wilkie had stolen her book and given it to MacMillan. After all, the man had been a journalist back in Sydney, so he was undoubtedly able to read her memos. As a result of the theft, she could not produce any notes before the court. When asked about the contents of the letter, Doust told Foster that it was a long letter and she could not recall exactly what the gist was.

Dorothy Doust's suspicions had been correct. It was MacMillan who pocketed her notebook and it was he who had sent a transcription of the impugned letter to Senator Pearce. But the letter was rather quickly swept away during the hearing as something the agitated Phillips had quite foolishly written in a fit of anger. The court deemed this action a moment of 'bad judgement' on Phillips' part written in a pique of anger and left it at that.[2]

Although no one could produce the telegram that Phillips had allegedly sent to Allen that same day telling him to disregard the letter, the court believed Phillips had come to his senses in time and had genuinely tried to correct his impulsive first reaction by sending the 'missing' telegram. To make sure that MacMillan would not come back and raise any more trouble, the court went on to hold him up for scrutiny. It appeared that MacMillan had a few ghosts hidden in the closet.

In May 1919, a soldier's body, that of Private Thomas Hamilton, was reported as having been identified. His relatives sent an amount of almost 25 pounds to ensure a headstone and an inscription. Because no trace of any payment into the AIF funds could be found, the court suspected MacMillan had fraudulently pocketed it. When Foster's inquiry dug further, they found a total amount of 62 pounds and 5 shillings in irregular amounts paid out by relatives to MacMillan over a period of months.[3] That sealed his fate; it meant that anything he might bring before the inquiry would be regarded as highly unreliable.

Sam MacMillan's financial transactions had been open to serious question at the first inquiry. There had been insufficient evidence to incriminate him at that time and therefore he had not been accused of any wrongdoing. He did not have to face a court martial but as part of the ongoing demobilisation of AIF men he was listed to be sent home; this meant he received all payments by the AIF due to him and could arrive in Australia without a disreputable record.

The new hearing revealed that there was now proof that MacMillan had forged the name of another officer on a receipt for money for the removal of a deceased soldier. Defeated, MacMillan backed down. Because Cecil Smith had not been summoned, much of MacMillan's written evidence was deemed as inadmissible due to 'hearsay'.

As a last resort, the journalist, determined to have the truth revealed, went to see Sir James Burns in Sydney. He desperately urged the old man to discuss the story with authorities who were unbiased and would listen. MacMillan also advised Burns to ask some trustworthy British authority to search for his son's remains.

Burns's health by now was very poor and he was as good as bedridden. As an old army man, he was also very aware of the consequences such action would have on the reputation of the military. He let MacMillan know that he was thoroughly disgusted with the whole business and that he would 'rather not reopen the wound'. James Burns died in 1923.[4]

Chapter 23
CONCLUSIONS

It had not been an easy road for Foster. Now that the inquiry had come to a close, he would need to write down his conclusions and findings. It had been clear almost from the start that no good would be served by obtaining a conviction against any of the men. Especially not against Phillips and Allen.

Replacing them would no doubt present huge difficulties.[1] Aspects of their conduct may have been questionable, but they had been instrumental in establishing and maintaining the Australian Graves Services in the field. They were familiar with all aspects of the job; they had established strong and commendable relationships with the British and both men were, on the surface of things, currently doing a reasonable job of leading their men.

For more than a year the inadequate functioning of the AGS had plagued Australia House and the AIF. It had all started with Will Bollen's letter in March 1920, accusing AGS administration in France and Belgium of lack of coordination and proper supervision.

After the first inquiry, Major Phillips had remained officer in charge of the AGS and Major Allen occupied the position of inspector. When Captain Meikle, a member of the court, was appointed OC in France, it fed the already existing suspicion that the members of that inquiry had been bribed.

New staffing arrangements for the AGS had been organised in May and by October 1920 General Birdwood was able to report that all ranks were working efficiently. But as newspaper articles about the wonderful work of the Australian Graves Services surfaced, Lee, MacMillan, Bollen and Gray had no intention of backing down and started venting their own version of the truth to newspapers and the authorities. Lee, especially, was out to wreak havoc. He had only been called to testify in Bollen's case and he felt his own accusations had not been properly investigated.

It was only when MacMillan wrote a letter to Senator Pearce revealing the hoaxing of Robert Burns's grave that Pearce demanded action and for another inquiry to be held in London, with further evidence to be examined in Australia. The charges being made were strong. In particular, the letter Phillips had sent to Allen requesting him to exhume the body immediately, before Smith arrived, had been quite incriminating.

Because Smith had not been called by the court to give evidence, MacMillan's accusations could be deemed as hearsay, thus making them inadmissible. Smith had eventually been allowed to be present at the exhumation so the court saw no reason to take action against either Phillips or Allen. The court did, however, note that Allen 'in his military capacity and beyond the fact that he holds rank as an Honorary Major, evidently has little knowledge of the service'.[2] The high commissioner, Andrew Fisher, had personally inquired into the exhumation matter and Smith's complaints; he reported that he thought Smith had no real grounds for grievance because all information given to him had been provided in good faith.[3]

It had been the second inquiry's obligation to reassess the findings of the first inquiry of March 1920. The new panel— Foster, Beavis and Whitham—had questioned Phillips and Allen about it; they in turn gave the same answers to the questions they had given to the first inquiry. The court found that the allegations made in London by Lee against Phillips were based on malice and were not supported by the facts. Lee would be formally notified that his complaints had been investigated and found to be unsubstantiated.

Realising he had held only half an inquiry, Foster was now ready to send the findings of his court back to Australia, where they were expecting to reassemble at a later date. But when the incomplete proceedings of the court were handed over to the defence department, Foster and the two other members of the inquiry, as well as the commanding officer of the AIF in London, Colonel Jackson, advised against yet another hearing.[4] Jackson claimed that a properly thorough hearing would present problems of a logistical and financial nature. Some witnesses now lived in Europe and those in Australia were widely dispersed, living in Western Australia, Victoria and New South Wales.

Assembling such a court would involve great costs and the nature of such an inquiry would be very distressing to relatives of the deceased soldiers, whose bodies, as a result, might need to be dug up as evidence.[5] The many witnesses required to take the stand would make it doubtful whether the inquiry and its outcome could be kept confidential. There was no indication that anyone outside the department was aware that an inquiry had been held in London and it was in the interests of all those involved to keep it that way.

It was advised that therefore the defence department should rely upon the good reputation of the court. Although the inquiry into the allegations of Bollen and Lee would remain incomplete if the inquiry wasn't resumed, Fisher thought the court had done enough.

The proceedings of the court were referred to Felix Cassel, the judge advocate-general of the Australian military forces in London.[6] Cassel was commonly known as the 'JAG'. Australia at the time did not have its own judge advocate-general, so although Cassel was the English JAG he was also the legal advisor to the AIF. His advice covered a wide range of issues dealing with administrative law, government contracting, civilian and military personnel law, law of war and international relations and environmental law, to name a few. He sometimes served as a prosecutor for the military when conducting courts martial and sometimes as a military judge in courts martial and courts of inquiry.

After due deliberation, the JAG deemed the proceedings to have been properly conducted and that the evidence justified the findings. Cassel submitted some observations, but these only referred to unimportant points. His report also stated that the evidence did not warrant further action.[7] In May 1921, Pearce agreed with Cassel's advice. In a letter to him he wrote: 'In view of the satisfactory nature of this report, I do not propose to take any further action in this case.'[8] There was no court inquiry into the case ever held in Australia and William Lee never got to ask Alfred Allen the questions he had written down. Although no doubt discouraged, he did not pursue the matter further and never sought contact with the press again.

New guidelines for the Australian Graves Services were now in the process of being executed and Foster was aware that the AGS would soon cease to exist. By mid-1921, fewer identifiable bodies were being discovered every month. Hoping to speed things up, in a race against time as identification would become more difficult as the months and years passed by, locals were asked to help find bodies, but the people of France and Belgium had become frustrated with the constant appeals to help find missing soldiers; they wanted to get on with their lives.

There were many reasons why multiple areas would always remain uncleared. The graves units had to deal with devastated terrains replete with the ruins of buildings, waterlogged and damaged roads, thick mud and unexploded bombs and shells. The weather conditions were often unfavourable and the ground was too broken. In the winter months its frozen state made digging impossible. Areas that were heavily wooded or excessively marshy were difficult to access and, with the numbers of volunteers diminishing fast, there were fewer hands to do the work. Working at a distance from the main road made transporting the bodies difficult. General service wagons pulled by mules or horses had to be used to transport the corpses to ambulances waiting on a road.

Private owners of the farmlands were getting fed up with having to report anything they found to exhumation units. They wanted to get on with their lives and reinstate themselves as farmers so made access to their land difficult for the British Grave Registration Units, who they regarded as bothersome.

In view of this, it was expected that the AGS would soon be absorbed into the Imperial War Graves Commission. This was expected to happen within months, and all men serving with the AGS would in the very near future be sent home. Taking all this into account, it appeared rather useless to embarrass the services and their men further by holding an inquiry in Australia. After Foster sent his report to Pearce, the matter was dropped.

In September 1921, just six months after Foster sent his findings to Australia, the Imperial War Graves Commission discussed taking over the Australian Graves Services. A statement was issued by Malcolm Lindsay Shepherd, the new representative of Australia on the IWGC, and published in the national newspapers.[9] He had been private secretary to successive prime ministers and had established a close relationship with all of them, especially with Andrew Fisher.

Shepherd informed parliament that he believed this new arrangement would be satisfactory to Australia and its people.[10] The British War Office was preparing the withdrawal of their units from actively searching the battlefields at the end of

September. The decision to take out the military units was also made due to financial motives. The AGS had cost the government a lot of money and, although there were still many soldiers missing, it was not expected that the benefits in the future would outweigh the cost. It would be easier and cheaper to incorporate a few Australian men into IWGC and pass the task on to them.

However, there were still many families with 'missing' loved ones. Most of them realised they would never be able to travel to France and, without proper Australian units to search the land, their hope of ever getting any closure was quickly diminishing. So it was no surprise that the proposed absorption of the Australian Graves Services into the IWGC created public controversy. To ease concern, the IWGC was quick to assure the public that there would be no discontinuation of exhumations and that a few Australians would stay employed to help identify any of their own found in the field.[11]

With 12,000 Australian corpses still scattered on the northern French battlefields, the public expressed extreme disappointment at the decision to terminate the active search for bodies. Most men discharged weren't sorry to leave, but they regretted that not all of those who had died would be buried in a decent grave. Many in Australia were disillusioned by the unexpected withdrawal and considered it a disturbing breach of promises once made.

Since the beginning of 1921 Prime Minister Billy Hughes had been considering discontinuing the service and by August 1921, as he prepared for a tour of inspection in France, he was still deliberating the matter because it was causing such controversy. For bereaved Australians, members of the AGS were their only battlefield representatives. The public feared they would have no one left to turn to after the demobilisation of the AGS. Members of the AGS in turn let the government know that they feared that 'the Australian interests could not be sufficiently guaranteed if all the work was left to the Imperial authorities whose personnel knew little of Australian affairs'.[12]

In London, a deputation of Australians met Shepherd at Australia House, demanding that Australian searching and exhumation should continue. Members of the AGS fed the protests, claiming that thousands of bodies could still be recovered if only the government would fulfil their obligations. Hughes responded by assuring the public that no reasonable costs would be spared to ensure that as many Australians as needed would be kept in France to protect and safeguard the interests and desires of the relatives of the fallen soldiers.

Shepherd in turn demanded that the IWGC take on five Australian staff members, to ensure that all means of identification were met and reburials were properly carried out. With the IWGC asserting its authority and taking control of the war cemeteries, Shepherd reassured the public that all 'Australian interests were safe with the IWGC', but that 'the need for a separate Australian Graves organization in France and Belgium will end'.[13]

By the end of 1921, 1250 Australian soldiers were still reported as missing in the Fromelles area alone. Over 60,000 Australians lost their lives during World War I; almost 50,000 died on the Western Front. Some 11,000 Australian soldiers are still missing in France. Their remains were never found.

Chapter 24

THE DISCOVERY AT PHEASANT WOOD
2009

In 1919 the German authorities had sent word to the Red Cross with regard to the location of Lieutenant Robert David Burns's body: to look for five mass graves located close to Pheasant Wood, near Fromelles. The Bavarians had carefully documented the site at the time of the burial. The Red Cross sent this information on to the Australian Graves Services, who sent it to Alfred Allen. Allen declared during the second inquiry that he had walked all around the area but had found no indication of a mass grave, although he was aware that the Germans often dug slit trenches to bury the dead.

Allen may not have been looking too enthusiastically into the probable presence of a mass grave because that would have meant a great deal of gruesome work. Digging up hundreds of bodies, identifying them and then reburying them could not have been very appealing.

However, his discovery of that particular grave would have

secured Allen a place in the history books. We will never know how Major Alfred Allen, the famous 'finder of missing men', could have overlooked such a large burial site. If he had actually walked around the area, as he claimed, he would have had difficulty in missing it, particularly given his great skills in identifying burial sites and finding lost bodies. History bypassed Alfred Allen in 1920 and the gravesite at Pheasant Wood remained unnoticed for almost ninety years, until Lambis Englezos, a Melbourne art teacher with a long interest in military history, finally located it with the help of historian Peter Barton. Following a visit to Fromelles in 2002, Englezos found a discrepancy between the numbers of unidentified soldiers buried compared to the lists of the missing. He suspected the missing bodies might be found in unmarked graves dug by the Germans. These graves had never been recovered but, when Barton examined the Bavarian World War I files in Munich, he got a good idea of where he should look. As he worked his way through the National Archives in London, he found British aerial photos from 1916 revealing three large open pits just before the forest and three closed ones. Englezos and Barton were certain these graves held Australian soldiers.

It was difficult for Englezos and Barton to get their message across to the authorities. They were told that a site that big could hardly have been missed by the British Graves Registration Units and the Australian Graves Services because their work during the post-war years had been so thorough. But the two men persisted; as evidence mounted, their case became strong enough to finally warrant an official investigation.

How the site could have been missed when military grave units searched these battlefield areas time and again in the aftermath of the war is still a bit of a mystery. Although it has become evident that the AGS suffered from mismanagement in the years 1919 to 1921, back in 1920 it was taken for granted that the bodies of many of those killed in battle would never be found. Even though Major Allen was identifying one body after another, many dead would remain in the ground. If the bodies had been buried deep enough they would not be discovered by a farmer's plough or members of the AGS prodding the soil and in some cases bodies had been blown to bits.

Pheasant Wood, or Bois du Faisan, lies very close to Fromelles—just across a field before the first village homes come into view. In 2009 this peaceful village became the setting for an enormous operation when the remains of 250 Australian and British soldiers were exhumed. It wasn't an easy task to uncover the bodies. The clay in the area was sticky, so sieving the earth to find anything tangible in the way of objects or bits of bone was useless. It came down to careful finger probing and using metal detectors. Nevertheless, the bodies were there and the German archives were proven to be totally accurate. In all those years no one had actually taken heed and so the burial pits at Pheasant Wood remained undisturbed for decades.

—■—

After the battle of Fromelles in 1916, the commander of the 21st Bavarian Reserve Infantry, General Julius Ritter von Braun, had ordered the digging of a mass grave behind Pheasant Wood, instructing his men how to go about the work of excavating large pits and arranging the dead in neat rows, one on top of the other. They had, however, removed almost every object of identification and sent them off to the Red Cross for the families of the slain men. But by 2009 there was a new method of identification: DNA.

The families of all the missing were asked to come forward and offer their DNA. Many did just that. To date, almost one hundred missing soldiers have been identified, including Lieutenant Robert David Burns.

Reported as missing on 20 July 1916 and commemorated on the Australian National Memorial at Villers-Bretonneux, Burns had been listed for decades as having 'No Known Grave'. But the remains of Robert Burns were finally discovered in that small patch of farmland on the outskirts of the northern French village of Fromelles. His body was subsequently identified through DNA in 2010.

The Pheasant Wood exhumations unearthed more than two hundred Australian bodies. When the work of recovering the bodies started and the first of the corpses appeared, Lambis Englezos was quoted as saying: 'G'day boys, I know it's been a long time but be patient, don't worry, we'll get you.' The remains of the fallen soldiers, including those of Robert Burns, were interred in a specially established Fromelles (Pheasant Wood) Military Cemetery in France.

Chapter 25
THE MYSTERIOUS MAJOR

During his life and for many years beyond, Major Alfred Allen's choices mystified and puzzled both his family and those with whom he became acquainted. Although he had built up an enviable reputation as an architect in Sydney, at the height of his career Alfred chose to leave Australia and abandon his wife and child in order to work in the relief service. Why did he decide to spend his life working in such difficult places under horrific conditions? What drove him to turn his back on his family and friends, and the life he had built for himself in Sydney?

When he left Australia for France in 1915, he left for good. He never saw his wife and daughter again. The only contact he maintained with his family was with Mary, his sister, who would receive a letter from him every now and again. The man whom writer John Oxenham called 'the discoverer of men' isn't easy to slot into a pigeonhole.

Young Alfred's father, after whom he had been named, had come to Australia from Belfast, Ireland in 1839 at the age of four when his father, William Bell Allen, moved his family to Sydney. William Allen, an enterprising man, set up a successful candle works factory and Alfred Allen senior became an apprentice to a firm of engineers in Sydney. William Allen was a New South Wales politician during the 1860s and Alfred senior too was always interested in politics. It was his Irish heritage, he claimed, and it would get him into trouble at times. The engineering firm where he first worked did not share his support for early closing hours at hotels and an eight-hour working day; they dismissed their young apprentice as a result of his resolute beliefs.

Alfred's father went on to have a varied career as an engineer, gold-digger, farmer, printer, manufacturer and insurance agent for the Australian Mutual Provident Society. After his grandfather, William Allen died, his own father maintained the soap and candle works for about 25 years and then sold out.

As a leading member of the Society of Friends (the Quakers), Alfred senior was active in philanthropic and other works; he was a life governor of Sydney Hospital and a founder of the Sydney Night Refuge and Soup Kitchen. However, he was regarded by some of the Friends as troublesome and was dismissed as their registrar in 1902 after the Devonshire Street Friends brought three charges against him—immorality, unsound doctrine and disorderly conduct.[1]

Alfred junior was the second son of Alfred Allen senior and his wife, Amelia Petford Allen; he was born at his parents' home in Victoria Street, Marrickville. On his birth certificate, his father's occupation was given as 'Sugar Planter'. Alfred Allen senior had left Sydney in November 1869 (just a few weeks before Alfred junior was born) to establish a sugar farm, known as 'Friends Farm', at Meridan Plains near Caloundra, Queensland.

Alfred Allen senior was evidently a very strong-minded, religious man and his purpose in going to Queensland appeared to be to establish a Friends community, away from the disputations that had occurred in Sydney. After two consecutive seasons of floods, however, he abandoned the idea of his own commune and returned to his wife, who he had left in Sydney to fend for herself with three very young children.

In Sydney, he found his way into politics and represented Paddington for seven years in the New South Wales Legislative Assembly (1887–94) and he was re-admitted as a member of the Friends in 1889. Alfred Allen senior had a somewhat volatile character and his career was certainly a stormy one.

Little is known of Alfred junior's childhood and adolescence. His mother, Amelia, played the organ at the Waverley Congregational Church and this is where Alfred married Ellen (Nellie) Renshaw, daughter of George William Renshaw and Mary Myers, in 1897.

Young Alfred had chosen a career as an architect. Being the son of a noted Quaker, he was asked to draw up the plans for the Devonshire Street Meeting House in Sydney.[2] This building which he designed for the Society of Friends was established with considerable financial support from the London branch of the Friends. But Allen senior, much to his son's dismay, created a scene when the building was opened and henceforth was banned from the premises for disorderly conduct. When Alfred senior showed up uninvited at some of the Friends' meetings there, the Friends decided to close the Meeting House and resorted to holding their meetings elsewhere so as to avoid any further confrontation with him.[3] Young Alfred, however, went on to establish himself as a noted architect; he drew up the plans for many residences, particularly on the North Shore of Sydney between 1902 and 1914, as well as for a number of bank buildings for the Bank of New South Wales.

Alfred's daughter and only child, Doris Eileen, was born in February 1900. Nevertheless, it soon became evident that his marriage with Nellie was not a happy one. His wife later told her family and others that he had had a strong desire to leave for Africa, accompanied by his family, to work as a Quaker missionary there, but she had not been at all happy about this plan and refused to go. As a result, he left Australia to travel around England and South Africa without his family.

After a year of journeying through Europe and Africa, he came back to Australia full of stories about how London's streets were kept clean by hosing them each night, and about the new King's College, which he found to be one of the twentieth century's greatest wonders of architectural brilliance with its perfect height, light and ventilation. In newspaper interviews he revealed an almost passionate excitement when he described the British railway system; he was impressed by its effectiveness in getting people from one end of the city to another in comfortable coaches and in such a short time. He did not hide his love of England, and London in particular.[4]

Alfred had applied to become a member of the Society of Friends in Sydney in 1912 and was accepted into membership 'by convincement'. Two years later World War I broke out and, seeming almost desperate to leave home, he applied in Sydney to join other young Quakers who had left Australia to work with the Society of Friends in London and Europe. The Quakers were pacifists, so he did not envisage engaging in combat.

At the end of 1916 *The Australian Friend*, a paper that featured articles about Australian Quakers working abroad, published a letter Alfred sent them about his work with Belgian refugees in the Netherlands in the previous two years. In it he described how hard it was to work in an environment where the people did not speak the same language and how poor the circumstances were in the refugee camp. In describing their celebration of Belgium Day and how he was asked to march at the head of their procession, he seemed eager to show that he had managed to steal the hearts of those poor souls in the camps. The scene he depicts is almost messianic—Alfred marching along and the children clinging to him as though he were the English version of the Pied Piper of Hamlin:

> The camp celebrated Belgium Day, and insisted on my marching with them, which I did, in front of the camp band, all through the city. The 400 kiddies sang their beloved Belgian songs, and waved their flags. I just love them all, and they hang on to their Englishman.[5]

Alfred Allen was evidently prone to vanity and often lied about his age and height on numerous official documents, leading people to believe he was younger and taller than he actually was.

On 5 August 1917, when Alfred returned to London from France, he received word that his father had died. Aged 78, Alfred senior had died suddenly of a heart condition at his home in Waverley. His father's will left his estate and his money to his daughter and two of his sons; Alfred junior got nothing and neither did Alfred senior's widow. Alfred senior had stated that his daughter and sons were to support their mother financially until she died, but a few months later Amelia Petford Allen went to court about the matter. The 'support' her children granted her was two pounds a week and she could barely make do, she let the judge know. The court granted her four pounds and the matter was settled, but her son Alfred never got a penny.[6]

From 1917 Alfred worked for the Red Cross in London, where he was 'gassed' badly during an attack on the city. After he recovered he was put in charge of the YMCA all-night motor rescue work in the darkened streets of London as the conflict wore on. Finally, at the end of the war, just as he was hoping for a brief rest, the Red Cross authorities appointed him as their shipping representative in England.

It was through his connections at the Red Cross that Alfred was asked to join the graves department of the AIF. The English author and publisher John Oxenham, a pseudonym for William Arthur Dunkerley, had become especially impressed with Alfred's work and his efforts. His admiration resulted in a glowing depiction of Alfred in his book *High Altars* about his travels across the battlefields of France and Flanders. Alfred never once openly objected to the unrealistic picture Oxenham's words portrayed.

Despite the scandals concerning missing Red Cross goods and the alleged hoaxing of the Robert Burns grave, Alfred stayed on as a member of the Australian Graves Services until 1922, when the Imperial War Graves Commission took over the work of the AGS. From 1922 to 1924 he continued to work for the IWGC.

After it became apparent that Alfred would not return to Australia, Nellie Renshaw Allen applied for a divorce in 1923 due to abandonment by her husband. Her application was effected in 1925 and she remarried in that same year.

After his discharge from the IWGC, Alfred Allen at last left for the country he had wanted to take his family to so many years before, South Africa. Taking up farming in the Transvaal, he stayed there for almost ten years, but returned to England when the Friends requested him to.

After undertaking voluntary work with the Friends' Allotments Committee's Allotments Gardens for the Unemployed scheme, Alfred was later asked to tour Suffolk and produce a report on the Quaker management in the area. In addition to that, it appeared that the Quaker administration housed at Glamorgan was causing problems. The management of thirteen Quaker groups and 50 individual societies there was considered too great a task for the person in charge. It was therefore suggested that Alfred Allen go there to help.

Not having a decent means of transport to travel the English countryside, Alfred turned to Lord Nuffield, the founder of Morris Motors Limited, asking him to donate a used car to the Quaker committee for him to use. To Alfred's surprise, Nuffield presented him with a special edition of the Morris Eight car.

In August 1936 Alfred wrote a sad letter to his brother Stanley Allen, letting him know that his health was deteriorating and that he feared the worst. Suffering from a malignant lump in his throat he had hardly been able to eat for months and as a result he had become terribly weak and thin. A specialist had sent him to hospital for x-rays and he feared this would result in an operation he might not survive.

He went on to ask his brother to allot a large portion of the 3000 pounds of his estate to his daughter, Doris, should he die. Stan was to go about this with utmost discretion without mentioning the name of the benefactor. In the letter, he referred to his wife and daughter as 'the Nellie and Doris affair, an unhappy period I shut out of my life years ago and no one has ever been told'.

Despising failure so much, Alfred had never told anyone abroad about his failed marriage, not even mentioning his child to a soul. The disappointment he felt about this episode was so great that he never mustered up enough courage to return 'home'. In his last letter to Stan, he let his brother know that he regretted never having seen them again and that he had often thought of saving up enough money to make the trip home.

On 23 October 1936, the Friends reported that Alfred Allen was lying seriously ill at the Nursing Home, Strangways Terrace, Truro, in Cornwall. Suffering from an incurable disease, the Friends let the outside world know that he was not expected to recover. Alfred Allen died just five days later on 28 October 1936.

The life of a strange, mysterious and ambiguous man had come to an end.[7]

ACKNOWLEDGEMENTS

I am grateful to:

Richard Walsh who went above and beyond.

Bob and Tom, who once again generously gave their time to weed out the first draft.

Rebecca Kaiser for brilliant support, feedback and for turning all the bits and bobs into an actual book.

Simone Ford, my copy editor, for wise and attentive remarks and impressive professionalism.

The staff at Allen & Unwin for their hard work.

Jacqueline Raillot for translating the French documents into English.

Jenny Madeline and Judy van Middeldyk who helped piece together the life of Alfred Allen.

The staff at the Tourist Office Poperinge for their aid at locating Bird Cage Camp.

The staff at The Fromelles (Pheasant Wood) Military Cemetery for their assistance and patience in helping me to find answers to many questions.

Kasper Koudenburg, my most important reader.

Jialu Zhang for being a wonderful person and a fabulous cook.

Jacqueline Loos and Hanneke Piederiet for cheering me on.

Anja and Luuk for many years of friendship.

And all the people I may have forgotten to mention.

Thank you all for helping me to turn this book into a far more readable one than I could have managed on my own.

NOTES

Much of the information for this book has come from one Commonwealth of Australia government source, 'Court of Inquiry: To inquire into and report upon certain matters in connection with the Australian Graves Services'. This 790-page report concerning the Australian Graves Services dates from 1920–21 and is available online at the National Archives of Australia, series number MP367/1, control symbol 446/10/1840 <https://naa12.naa.gov.au/SearchNRetrieve/Interface/ViewImage. aspx?B=362638&S=1>. It will be referred to in the notes as 'NAA: MP367/1, 446/10/1840' followed by a page number.

Abbreviations
AWM   Australian War Memorial
NAA   National Archives of Australia

CHAPTER 1 ROBERT DAVID BURNS

1 Peter Barton, *The Lost Legions of Fromelles*, Allen & Unwin, Sydney, 2014, pp. 188–9.

CHAPTER 2 HOW IT CAME ABOUT

1 Imperial War Graves Commission, NAA: A458, P337/6 PART 1.
2 Defence, Imperial War Graves Commission, Minutes of proceedings, NAA: A458, P337/6 ATTACHMENT 1, p. 356.
3 'Australian graves in France', *The Age*, 3 November 1920, p. 6.
4 The Australia House story, NAA: A463, 1966/2350.
5 NAA: SPEDDING Quentin Shaddock, B2455, item number 8093062.
6 Iain Gordon, *Lifeline: A British casualty clearing station on the Western Front, 1918*, The History Press, Stroud, UK, 2013, p. 56.
7 NAA: MP367/1, 446/10/1840, p. 382.
8 NAA: MP367/1, 446/10/1840, p. 380–418.
9 NAA: MP367/1, 446/10/1840, p. 380–418.
10 10 NAA: MP367/1, 446/10/1840, p. 158.
11 Australian Imperial Force unit war diaries, 1914–18 War—AWM4 Subclass 25/1—Director of Mechanical Transport Services, AIF AWM4 25/1/26—November—December 1919 Accession number: AWM RCDIG1014931.
12 MP367/1, 446/10/1840, p. 648.

CHAPTER 3 WILLIAM LEE

1 NAA: MP367/1, 446/10/1840, p. 425.
2 NAA: B2455 LEE William, item 8197334.
3 NAA: B2455, LEE William, p. 13.
4 NAA: B2455, LEE William, p. 29.
5 AWM, 2DRL/0598.
6 NAA: MP367/1, 446/10/1840, p. 469.
7 Bart Ziino, *A Distant Grief: Australians, war graves and the Great War*, University of Western Australia Press, Crawley, WA, 2007, pp. 84–5.
8 NAA: MP367/1, 446/10/1840, p. 347.

9 Australian Imperial Force unit war diaries, 1914–18 War—AWM4 Subclass 25/1 Director of Mechanical Transport Services, AIF AWM4 25/1/26—November—December 1919 Accession number: AWM RCDIG1014931.

10 NAA: MP367/1, 446/10/1840, p. 348.

11 Jane Tolerton, *Ettie: A life of Ettie Rout*, Penguin Books Australia, Ringwood, 1992.

12 NAA: MP367/1, 446/10/1840, p. 348.

13 NAA: MP367/1, 446/10/1840, p. 345.

14 NAA: MP367/1, 446/10/1840, p. 354.

15 NAA: MP367/1, 446/10/1840, p. 347.

CHAPTER 4 ALLEN CHARLES WATERS KINGSTON

1 NAA: B2455 KINGSTON Allen Charles Waters, item 7373109.

2 NAA: B2455 KINGSTON Allen Charles Waters.

3 <www.awm.gov.au/about/our-work/publications/contact/frank-hurley>.

4 Robert Dixon and Christopher Lee (eds), *The Diaries of Frank Hurley, 1912–1941*, Anthem Press, London, 2011, p. 76.

5 NAA: MP367/1, 446/10/1840, p. 383.

6 NAA: MP367/1, 446/10/1840, p. 383.

7 NAA: MP367/1, 446/10/1840, p. 3 (Kingston's letter).

8 NAA: MP367/1, 446/10/1840, p. 250.

9 Keith Jeffrey, *1916: A global history*, Bloomsbury Publishing, London, 2015, p. 250.

10 P.B. Clayton, *Tales of Talbot House*, Wentworth Press, Sydney, 2016, p. 25, p. 166.

11 NAA: MP367/1, 446/10/1840, p. 374.

12 NAA: MP367/1, 446/10/1840, p. 250.

CHAPTER 5 WILLOUGHBY RICHARD BOLLEN

1 NAA: B2455, BOLLEN Willoughby Richard, item 3096417.

2 NAA: MP367/1, 446/10/1840, p. 254.

3 NAA: MP367/1, 446/10/1840, p. 333.

4 NAA: MP367/1, 446/10/1840, p. 254.

5 NAA: MP367/1, 446/10/1840, p. 336.

6   NAA: MP367/1, 446/10/1840, p. 337.
7   NAA: MP367/1, 446/10/1840, p. 337.
8   NAA: MP367/1, 446/10/1840, p. 267.
9   NAA: MP367/1, 446/10/1840, p. 333.
10   NAA: MP367/1, 446/10/1840, p. 334.
11   NAA: MP367/1, 446/10/1840, p. 334.

CHAPTER 6 GEORGE LORT PHILLIPS

1   NAA: B2455, PHILLIPS George Lort, item 1989219.
2   NAA: B2455, PHILLIPS George Lort.
3   Bruce Scates, *Return to Gallipoli: Walking the battlefields of the Great War*, Cambridge University Press, Cambridge, 2006, p. 37; 'Gallipoli graves', *The Examiner*, 23 December 1918, p. 5.
4   Dudley McCarthy, *Gallipoli to the Somme: The story of C.E.W. Bean*, John Ferguson, Sydney, 1983, p. 367.
5   Proceedings court-martial, BOYCE Patrick Joseph (Sergeant), D'ELMAINE Jack (2nd Corporal), BYRON James (Private), O'NEILL Raymond George, SIMPSON Alexander (Private) Date of Court Martial—26 September 1919, NAA: A471, 7971, item 274505.
6   David A. Day, *Andrew Fisher: Prime Minister of Australia*, HarperCollins, Sydney, 2015.
7   NAA: MP367/1, 446/10/1840, p. 304.
8   NAA: MP367/1, 446/10/1840, p. 407.
9   NAA: MP367/1, 446/10/1840, p. 397.
10   NAA: MP367/1, 446/10/1840, p. 368.
11   NAA: MP367/1, 446/10/1840, p. 407.
12   NAA: MP367/1, 446/10/1840, pp. 491–4.
13   NAA: MP367/1, 446/10/1840, p. 400.
14   NAA: MP367/1, 446/10/1840, p. 364.
15   NAA: MP367/1, 446/10/1840, p. 363.
16   NAA: MP367/1, 446/10/1840, p. 353.

CHAPTER 7 ALFRED ALLEN

1   NAA: MP367/1, 446/10/1840, p. 380.

2 Alfred Allen (edited by Jim Smith), 'A correct and faithful
account of a journey to the "Fish River Caves" by the "Pickwick
Corresponding Club" in 1886', Blue Mountains Conservation
Society, *Hut News*, no. 298, November 2012, p. 4.

3 Vluchtoord Gouda door Martin Kraaijestein, 'Belgische
vluchtelingen in Gouda tijdens de Eerste Wereldoorlog', <http://
www.wereldoorlog1418.nl/vluchtelingen/kamp-gouda/>.

4 'Friends at the front', *The Sydney Morning Herald*, 2 May 1916,
p. 10.

5 'Quakers at the front', *The Sydney Morning Herald*, 17 March
1916, p. 4.

6 NAA: MP367/1, 446/10/1840, pp. 491–4 (p. 1).

7 Lena Lear, Inquiry regarding whereabouts of husband, NAA:
A2487, 1920/4208, item 210455.

8 Sir John Monash, Personal Files Book 23, 1 June–23 September
1919, Notes on Conference held at Victoria Street London,
Re Question of Desertion of Wives of Returned Soldiers,
AWM Accession number RCDIG0000643.

9 NAA: MP367/1, 446/10/1840, p. 419.

10 NAA: MP367/1, 446/10/1840, pp. 491–4.

11 NAA: MP367/1, 446/10/1840, pp. 491–4.

12 NAA: MP367/1, 446/10/1840, pp. 491–4.

13 Elien Raes, 'Bier, hop en de Eerste Wereldoorlog', Katholieke
Hogeschool Vives, Torhout Belgium, 2014.

CHAPTER 8 THE UGLY JOB

1 Bart Ziino, *A Distant Grief: Australians, war graves and the Great
War*, University of Western Australia Press, Crawley, WA, 2007, p. 88.

2 Red Cross, YMCA, Australian Comforts Fund and Australian
Graves Detachment—Correspondence, reports, etc to and from
Miss Rose Venn-Brown. Series number: AWM27, item 1090077.

3 Ziino, *A Distant Grief*, p. 91.

4 Venn-Brown, Rose (Civilian, YMCA and Red Cross) Diary Rose
Venn-Brown, 12 June 1919, AWM Accession number 2DRL0598.

5 Diaries of graves detachment digger William Frampton McBeath
in the years 1918–1919 of World War One, Letter from Will

McBeath to his mother, 19 April 1919, State Library of Victoria <http://handle.slv.vic.gov.au/10381/81498>.

6 NAA: B2455, JACKSON Alfred, item: 7362285.

CHAPTER 9 THE INQUIRY IN FRANCE

1 NAA: MP367/1, 446/10/1840, pp. 251–4, 397.
2 NAA: MP367/1, 446/10/1840, p. 293.
3 NAA: MP367/1, 446/10/1840, p. 697.
4 NAA: MP367/1, 446/10/1840, p. 295.
5 NAA: MP367/1, 446/10/1840, pp. 290, 295, 298.
6 NAA: MP367/1, 446/10/1840, pp. 290, 295, 296.
7 NAA: MP367/1, 446/10/1840, p. 289.
8 NAA: MP367/1, 446/10/1840, p. 252.
9 NAA: MP367/1, 446/10/1840, p. 316.
10 NAA: MP367/1, 446/10/1840, pp. 293–4.
11 NAA: MP367/1, 446/10/1840, pp. 296, 298.
12 NAA: MP367/1, 446/10/1840, p. 251.
13 NAA: MP367/1, 446/10/1840, p. 251.
14 NAA: MP367/1, 446/10/1840, p. 292.

CHAPTER 10 THE COURT IN LONDON

1 NAA: MP367/1, 446/10/1840, p. 572.
2 NAA: MP367/1, 446/10/1840, p. 572.
3 NAA: MP367/1, 446/10/1840, p. 134.
4 NAA: MP367/1, 446/10/1840, p. 351.
5 NAA: MP367/1, 446/10/1840, p. 353.
6 NAA: MP367/1, 446/10/1840, p. 129.
7 NAA: MP367/1, 446/10/1840, p. 128.
8 NAA: MP367/1, 446/10/1840, p. 354.
9 NAA: MP367/1, 446/10/1840, p. 276.
10 NAA: MP367/1, 446/10/1840, pp. 122–8.
11 NAA: MP367/1, 446/10/1840, p. 381.
12 NAA: MP367/1, 446/10/1840, p. 381.
13 NAA: MP367/1, 446/10/1840, p. 410.
14 NAA: MP367/1, 446/10/1840, p. 381

CHAPTER 11 RE-ESTABLISHING THE AGS

1 Official History, 1914–18 War: Records of Charles E. W. Bean, AWM38 Control symbol: 3DRL606/117/2 Item: 487464.
2 Diaries of graves detachment digger William Frampton McBeath in the years 1918–1919 of World War One, Letter from Will McBeath to his mother, 19 April 1919, p. 36, State Library of Victoria <http://handle.slv.vic.gov.au/10381/81498>.
3 NAA: MP367/1, 446/10/1840, p. 251.
4 Peter Barton, *The Lost Legions of Fromelles*, Allen & Unwin, Sydney, 2014, p. 375.
5 NAA: MP367/1, 446/10/1840, p. 614.
6 NAA: MP367/1, 446/10/1840, p. 14.
7 NAA: MP367/1, 446/10/1840, p. 702.
8 NAA: Hobbs, Joseph John Talbot (General, Sir, b. 1864 d. 1938), KCB, KCMG, VD, GOC Aust Corps Accession number: AWM 3DRL/2600.
9 NAA: MP367/1, 446/10/1840, p. 49.
10 Letter from Percy Buckley to Thomas Trumble, 2 March 1921, NAA:MP367/1, 446/10/1840 p. 3.

CHAPTER 12 ROCKING THE BOAT

1 'Australian graves in France', *The Age*, 10 November 1920, p. 11.
2 NAA: MP367/1, 446/10/1840, pp. 84–6.
3 NAA: MP367/1, 446/10/1840, pp. 122–8.
4 *The Sydney Morning Herald*, 7 February 1920, p. 7.
5 *The Sydney Morning Herald*, 7 February 1920, p. 7.
6 NAA: B2455 BIRDWOOD W R, item 4028769.
7 Sir George Pearce Personal Papers Birdwood Correspondence 1917–1937, NAA: A4719, 13, item 238602.
8 Ashley Ekins, *1918 Year of Victory: The end of the Great War and the shaping of history*, Exisle Publishing, Wollombi, NSW, 2010, p. 112.

CHAPTER 13 THE BODY DIVINER

1 John Oxenham, *Visitation of Graves in France and Flanders Garden City*, Forgotten Books, London, 2016, p. 3.

2 Bart Ziino, *A Distant Grief: Australians, war graves and the Great War*, University of Western Australia Press, Crawley, WA, 2007, pp. 179–8.

3 'Saviours of Amiens', *The Advertiser*, 9 November 1920, p. 7.

4 Ziino, *A Distant Grief*, p. 164.

5 War graves—visits to. Part 1, NAA: A1608, F27/1/7 Part 1.

6 'Tours to the battlefields', *The World's News*, 11 September 1920, p. 11.

7 'Visiting soldiers' graves', *The Herald* (Melbourne), 2 February 1920, p. 10.

8 Isabel Ramsey, 'To the memory of the Australian dead', *Sunday Times*, 6 February 1921, p. 3.

9 'Unknown dead', *The Daily Herald*, 3 January 1921, p. 5, <nla.gov.au/nla.news-article107246682>.

10 Matthew Stuart Smith, 'The relationship between Australians and the overseas graves of the First World War', thesis in the Humanities Program, Queensland University of Technology, 2010, p. 46.

11 Bruce Scates, *Return to Gallipoli: Walking the battlefields of the Great War*, Cambridge University Press, Cambridge, 2006, pp. 58–9.

12 *Maitland Daily Mercury*, 17 January 1921, p. 5.

13 NAA: Title: Graves. Visit of Mr [Stanley Melbourne] Bruce. Includes photographs of Major Allen of Australian War Graves Commission, NAA: A458, R337/7, item 87607.

14 NAA: MP367/1, 446/10/1840, p. 382.

15 NAA: MP367/1, 446/10/1840, p. 648.

16 NAA: MP367/1, 446/10/1840, p. 645.

17 NAA: MP367/1, 446/10/1840, p. 625.

CHAPTER 14 THE COLONEL'S SON

1 NAA: B2455, BURNS R.D. p. 14.

2 Red Cross Wounded and Missing file, AWM Accession number: 1DRL/0428.

3   G.J. Abbott and H.J. Gibbney, 'Burns, Sir James (1846–1923)', *Australian Dictionary of Biography*, vol. 7, Melbourne University Press, Carlton, Victoria, 1979.

4   Red Cross Wounded and Missing file, AWM Accession number: 1DRL/0428.

5   John Rickard, 'White, Vera Deakin (1891–1978)', *Australian Dictionary of Biography*, vol. 16, Melbourne University Press, Carlton, 2002.

6   Chomley, Mary Elizabeth Maud First World War, 1914–1918, AWM Accession number: 1DRL/0615.

7   Chomley, Mary Elizabeth Maud First World War, 1914–1918, AWM Accession number 1DRL615 [749/19/20] folder 2.

8   Red Cross Wounded and Missing file, AWM Accession number: 1DRL/0428.

CHAPTER 15 TAKING ACTION

1   NAA: MP367/1, 446/10/1840, p. 649.

2   NAA: MP367/1, 446/10/1840, p. 36.

3   NAA: MP367/1, 446/10/1840, p. 649.

4   Peter E. Hodgkinson, *Clearing the Dead*, Birmingham University Centre for First World War Studies, September 2007, <http://www.vlib.us/wwi/resources/clearingthedead.html>.

5   NAA: MP367/1, 446/10/1840, p. 625.

6   NAA: MP367/1, 446/10/1840, p. 639.

7   NAA: MP367/1, 446/10/1840, p. 549.

8   NAA: MP367/1, 446/10/1840, p. 37.

9   NAA: MP367/1, 446/10/1840, pp. 36–8.

10 NAA: MP367/1, 446/10/1840, p. 631.

CHAPTER 16 THE ALLEGED HOAX

1   'AIF graves', *Maitland Daily Mercury*, 17 January 1921, p. 5.

2   'General Birdwood', *The Examiner* (Launceston), 14 October 1920, p. 6; NAA: MP367/1, 446/10/1840, p. 11.

3   'Australian graves in France', *The Age*, 3 November 1920, p. 6.

4   NAA: MP367/1, 446/10/1840, p. 556.

5 NAA: MP367/1, 446/10/1840, p. 556.
6 'Graves of Australians', *Weekly Times*, 6 November 1920, p. 41.
7 'Australians' graves', *The Register*, 2 November 1920, p. 5.
8 NAA: MP367/1, 446/10/1840, p. 37.

CHAPTER 17 CROSSING THE CHANNEL

1 NAA: MP367/1, 446/10/1840, pp. 676–7.
2 NAA: MP367/1, 446/10/1840, pp. 549–50.
3 NAA: MP367/1, 446/10/1840, pp. 365–7.
4 NAA: MP367/1, 446/10/1840, p. 631.
5 NAA: MP367/1, 446/10/1840, p. 550.
6 NAA: MP367/1, 446/10/1840, p. 38.
7 NAA: MP367/1, 446/10/1840, p. 38.
8 NAA: MP367/1, 446/10/1840, pp. 38–9.
9 NAA: MP367/1, 446/10/1840, p. 556.
10 NAA: MP367/1, 446/10/1840, p. 39.
11 NAA: MP367/1, 446/10/1840, p. 651.
12 NAA: MP367/1, 446/10/1840, p. 631.
13 NAA: MP367/1, 446/10/1840, p. 562.
14 NAA: MP367/1, 446/10/1840, p. 562.
15 NAA: MP367/1, 446/10/1840, p. 550.

CHAPTER 18 SAM MacMILLAN

1 NAA: MP367/1, 446/10/1840, p. 36.
2 NAA: MP367/1, 446/10/1840, p. 637.
3 NAA: MP367/1, 446/10/1840, p. 37.
4 NAA: MP367/1, 446/10/1840, p. 37.
5 NAA: MP367/1, 446/10/1840, pp. 39–40.
6 NAA: MP367/1, 446/10/1840, p. 631.

CHAPTER 19 WILLIAM JAMES FOSTER

1 NAA: MP367/1, 446/10/1840, p. 35.
2 Sir George Pearce Personal Papers Birdwood Correspondence
   1917–1937 NAA A4719, 13, item 238602.
3 NAA: MP367/1, 446/10/1840, p. 3.

4 NAA: B2455, MCFARLANE Percy Muir, item 1943566.

5 NAA: MP367/1, 446/10/1840, p. 32.

6 NAA: B2455, FOSTER William James, item 4023625; H.J. Coates, 'Foster, William James (1881–1927)', *Australian Dictionary of Biography*, vol. 8, Melbourne University Press, Carlton, 1979.

CHAPTER 20 THE SECOND INQUIRY

1 NAA: MP367/1, 446/10/1840, p. 544.

2 NAA: MP367/1, 446/10/1840, p. 548.

3 NAA: MP367/1, 446/10/1840, p. 548.

4 NAA: MP367/1, 446/10/1840, p. 158.

5 NAA: MP367/1, 446/10/1840, pp. 158–9.

6 NAA: MP367/1, 446/10/1840, p. 549.

7 NAA: MP367/1, 446/10/1840, p. 550.

8 NAA: MP367/1, 446/10/1840, pp. 39–40.

CHAPTER 21 AN EMPTY GRAVE

1 NAA: MP367/1, 446/10/1840, p. 556.

2 NAA: MP367/1, 446/10/1840, pp. 559–60.

3 NAA: MP367/1, 446/10/1840, p. 656.

CHAPTER 22 STEALING NOTES

1 NAA: MP367/1, 446/10/1840, p. 566.

2 NAA: MP367/1, 446/10/1840, p. 606.

3 NAA: MP367/1, 446/10/1840, pp. 25, 31.

4 NAA: MP367/1, 446/10/1840, p. 39.

CHAPTER 23 CONCLUSIONS

1 NAA: MP367/1, 446/10/1840, p. 21.

2 NAA: MP367/1, 446/10/1840, p. 546.

3 NAA: MP367/1, 446/10/1840, p. 28.

4 NAA: MP367/1, 446/10/1840, p. 21.

5 NAA: MP367/1, 446/10/1840, p. 21.

6 NAA: MP367/1, 446/10/1840, p. 692.

7 NAA: MP367/1, 446/10/1840, p. 691.

8   NAA: MP367/1, 446/10/1840, p. 536.
9   'Australian graves', *The Observer* (Adelaide), 14 May 1921, p. 33; 'War graves commission', *Kalgoorlie Miner*, 7 September 1921, p. 1.
10 'Imperial Graves Commission', *The Ballarat Star*, 20 October 1921, p. 1.
11 'Australian grave', *The Gloucester Advocate*, 15 October 1921, p. 2.
12 Bart Ziino, *A Distant Grief: Australians, war graves and the Great War*, University of Western Australia Press, Crawley, WA, 2007, p. 102.
13 'Exhumation of bodies', *Barrier Miner* (Broken Hill), 20 October 1921, p. 1; Ziino, *A Distant Grief*, p. 104.

CHAPTER 25 THE MYSTERIOUS MAJOR

1   'Morris Family Papers, 1715–1925', coll. no. 1008, Haverford College Library, Haverford, PA 19041, USA <http://library.haverford.edu/file-id-774>.
2   'Society of Friends New Meeting House' *The Daily Telegraph*, 19 September 1903, p. 10.
3   William Nicolle Oats, 'Quakers in Australia in the nineteenth century', thesis, University of Tasmania, Hobart, 1982, p. 320, <eprints.utas.edu.au/17622/1/oats_vol_1.pdf>.
4   'Electrical cooking', *Tweed Daily* (Murwillumbah), 29 May 1914, p. 2; 'Where Britain leads' *Daily Telegraph* (Launceston), 2 June 1914, p. 7.
5   Alfred Allen, 'Our men in the field', *The Australian Friend*, 16 August 1916.
6   'Testators' family maintenance', *The Sydney Morning Herald*, 4 May 1918.
7   My grateful thanks to Jenny Madeline, archivist of the Quaker Meeting House in Sydney, and Alfred Allen's great-granddaughter Judy van Middeldyk for their kind and generous help in piecing together Alfred Allen's history in this chapter.

SELECT BIBLIOGRAPHY

Alfred Allen (edited by Jim Smith), 'A correct & faithful account of a journey to the "fish river caves" by the "Pickwick Corresponding Club" in 1886', Blue Mountains Conservation Society, *Hut News*, no. 298, November 2012 <bluemountains.org.au/documents/hutnews/richer/1211news_rich.pdf>.

Peter Barton, *The Lost Legions of Fromelles*, Allen & Unwin, Sydney, 2014.

Peter Bastian, *Andrew Fisher: An underestimated man*, University of NSW Press Ltd, Sydney, 2009.

Chrisje Brants and Kees Brants, *Velden van Weleer*, Nijgh&Van Ditmar, Amsterdam, 1993.

P. B. Clayton, *Tales of Talbot House: Everyman's club in Poperinghe and Ypres, 1915–18*, Wentworth Press, Sydney, 2016.

David Crane, *Empires of the Dead: How one man's vision led to the creation of WWI's War graves*, HarperCollins, London, 2013.

David A. Day, *Andrew Fisher, Prime Minister of Australia*, HarperCollins Publishers, Sydney, 2015.

Robert Dixon, *Photography, Early Cinema and Colonial Modernity: Frank Hurley's synchronized lecture entertainments*, Anthem Press, London, 2013.

Robert Dixon and Christopher Lee (eds) *The Diaries of Frank Hurley 1912–1941*, Anthem Press, London, 2011.

Ashley Ekins, *1918, Year of Victory: The end of the Great War and the shaping of history*, Exisle Publishing, Wollombi, NSW, 2010.

Iain Gordon, *Lifeline: A British casualty clearing station on the Western Front, 1918*, The History Press, Gloucestershire, 2013.

Jeremy Gordon-Smith, *Photographing the Fallen: A war graves photographer on the Western Front 1915–1919*, Pen & Sword Military, Barnsley, 2017.

Peter E. Hodgkinson, 'Clearing the Dead', *Centre for First World War Studies*, Sept. 2007, vol. 3:1, Birmingham University.

Keith Jeffrey, *1916: A global history*, Bloomsbury Publishing London, 2015.

Patrick Lindsay, *Fromelles: Australia's darkest day and the dramatic recovery of our fallen World War One diggers*, Hardie Grant Books, Melbourne, 2008.

Dudley McCarthy, *Gallipoli to the Somme: The story of C.E.W. Bean*, John Ferguson, Sydney, 1983.

Alasdair McGregor, *Frank Hurley: A photographer's life*, Penguin Books, Ringwood, 2009.

William Oats, 'Quakers in Australia in the Nineteenth Century', thesis, University of Tasmania, 1982, <http://eprints.utas.edu.au/17622/1/oats_vol_1.pdf>.

John Oxenham, '*High Altars: Visitation of Graves in France and Flanders*, Forgotten Books London, 2016 (originally published in 1918 by George H. Doran Company).

Antoine Prost, 'Les cimetières militaires de la Grande Guerre, 1914–1940', *Le Mouvement Social*, April 2011, La Découverte Paris.

Ellen Raes, 'Bier Hop en de Eerste Wereldoorlog', thesis, Katholieke Hogeschool Vives Torhout Belgium 2014.

Peter Rees, *Bearing Witness: The remarkable life of Charles Bean*, Allen & Unwin, Sydney, 2015.

Bruce Scates, *Return to Gallipoli: Walking the battlefields of the Great War*, Cambridge University Press, Cambridge, 2006.

Matthew Stuart Smith, 'The Relationship between Australians and the overseas graves of the First World War', thesis, Humanities Program Queensland University of Technology, Brisbane, 2010.

Jane Tolerton, *Ettie: A life of Ettie Rout*, Penguin Books, Ringwood, 1992.

Graham Wilson, *Accommodating the King's Hard Bargain: Military detention in the Australian Army 1914–1947*, Big Sky Publishing, Sydney, 2016.

Bart Ziino, *A Distant Grief: Australians, war graves and the Great War*, University of Western Australia Press, Crawley, WA, 2007.

INDEX